CATTITUDE

CATTITUDE

Your Cat Doesn't Give a F***
and Neither Should You

KATIE ABEY

HarperCollins*Publishers*

HarperCollins*Publishers*
1 London Bridge Street
London SE1 9GF

www.harpercollins.co.uk

HarperCollins*Publishers*
1st Floor, Watermarque Building,
Ringsend Road, Dublin 4, Ireland

First published by HarperCollins*Publishers*
2022

10 9 8 7 6 5 4 3 2 1

© Katie Abey 2022

Katie Abey asserts the moral right to be
identified as the author of this work

A catalogue record of this book is available
from the British Library

ISBN 978-0-00-852800-3

Printed and bound in Latvia

For more information visit:
www.harpercollins.co.uk/green

Dedicated to
Francis Von
Squiggleface
(the Third)

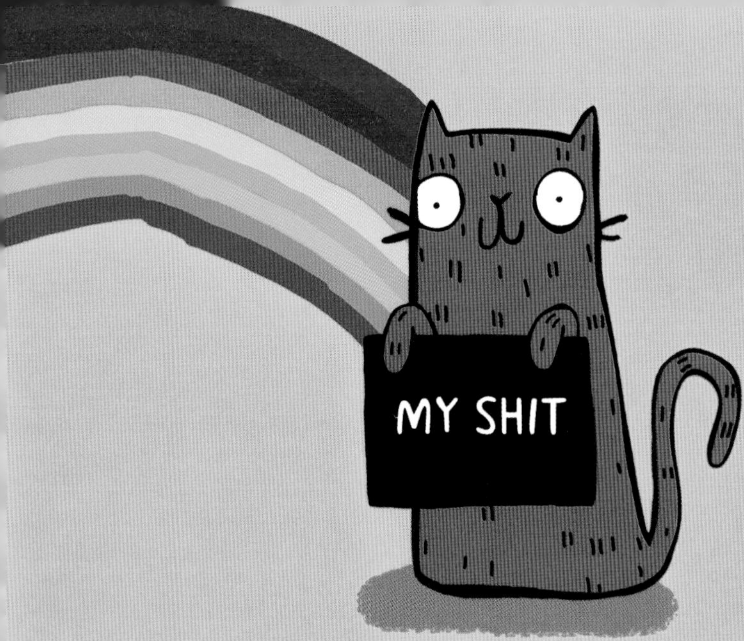
MY SHIT

The cats of the world stopped giving a fuck a very long time ago and have been giving off the right kind of energy for centuries. They saunter into every room with a level of confidence humans can only dream of. Kitties prioritise rest and their own happiness and just do not put up with the bullshit of others.

A clowder of sassy, sweary kitties have come together in book form to encourage you to rediscover your own self-belief. Standing strong in your boundaries and napping more often are the overall vibes you can expect here. With mantras such as 'Some people are just dickheads', 'Focus on the shit you can control' and 'Fuckin' look after yourself', you'll soon find yourself thinking, 'How would a cat react in this situation?'

It's time to channel some cattitude into your life decisions and start feeling more purroud of who you are.

YOUR SHIT

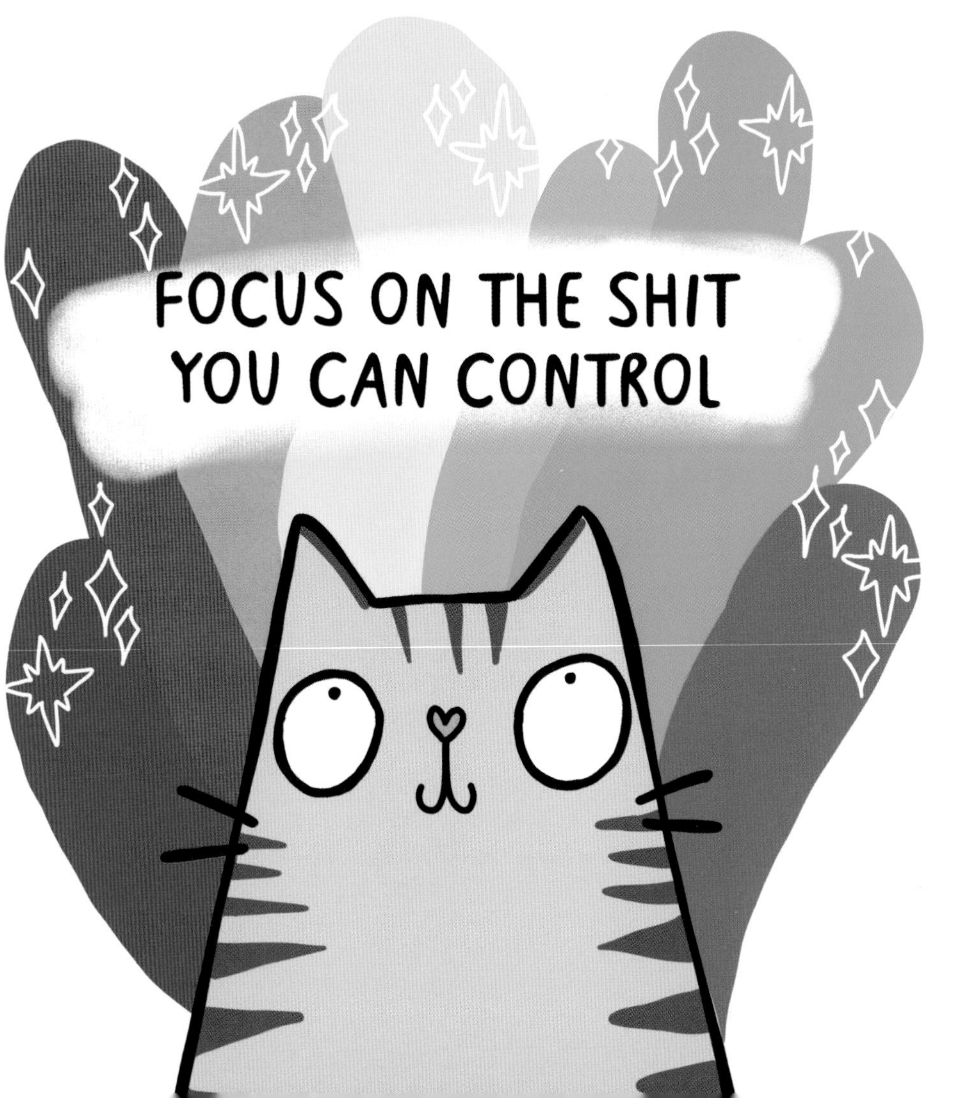
FOCUS ON THE SHIT
YOU CAN CONTROL

SHINE SO BRIGHT
THAT THOSE BITCHES
NEED SUNGLASSES

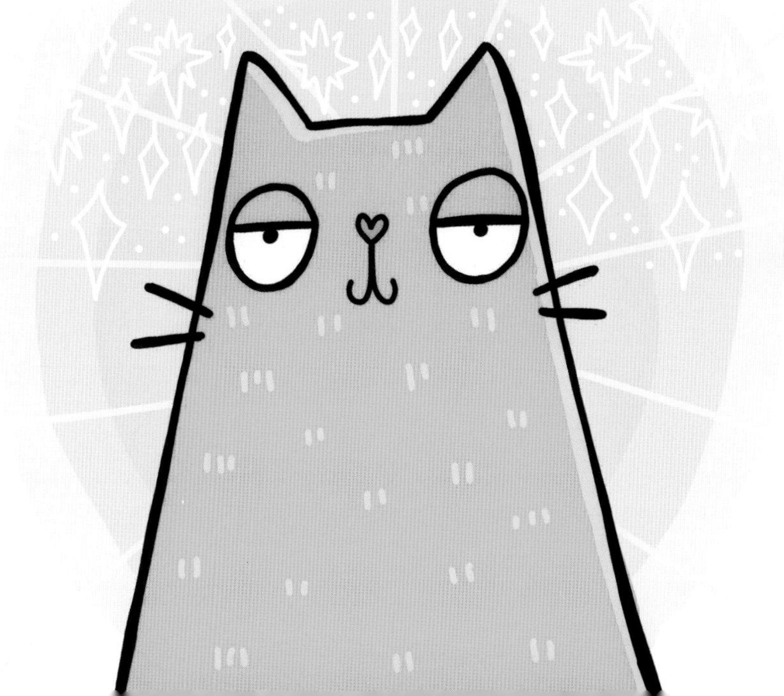

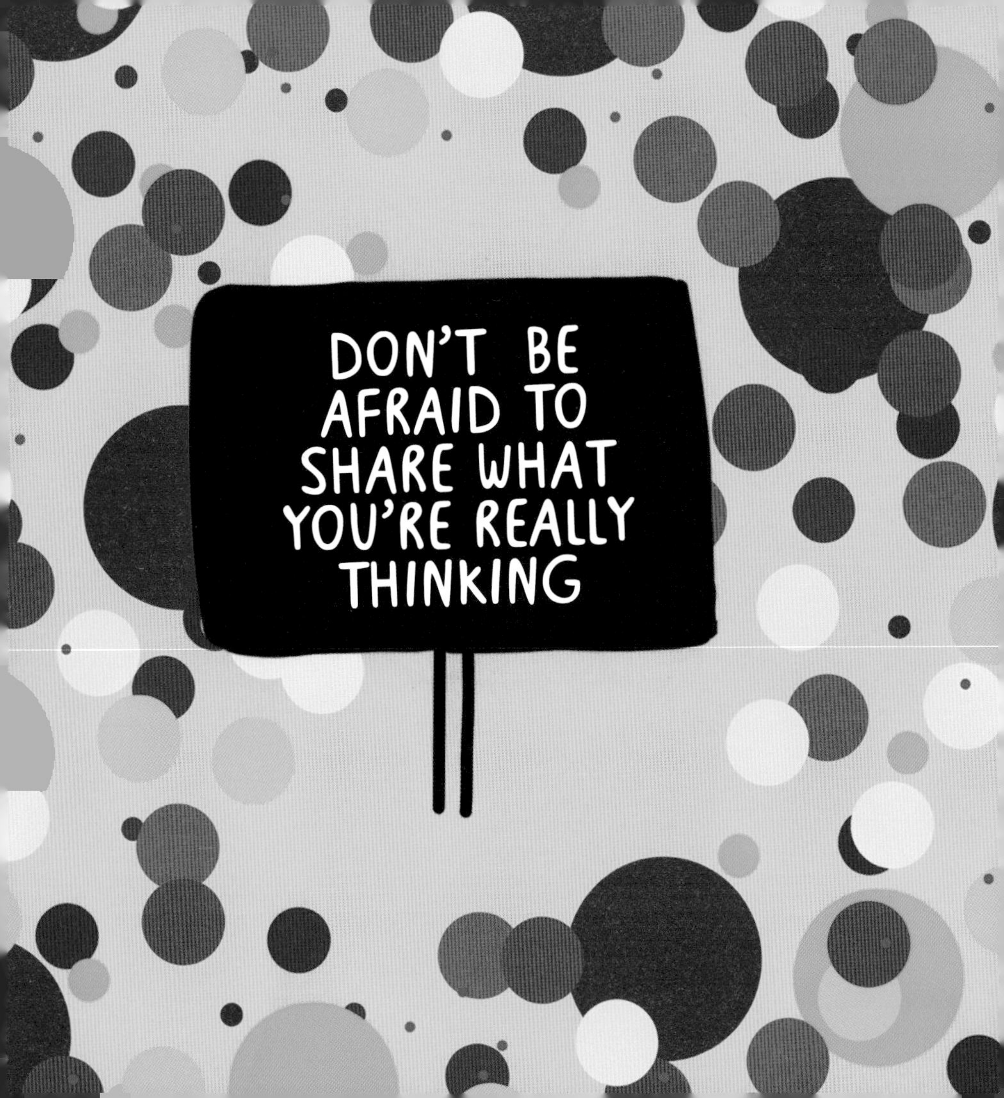
DON'T BE
AFRAID TO
SHARE WHAT
YOU'RE REALLY
THINKING

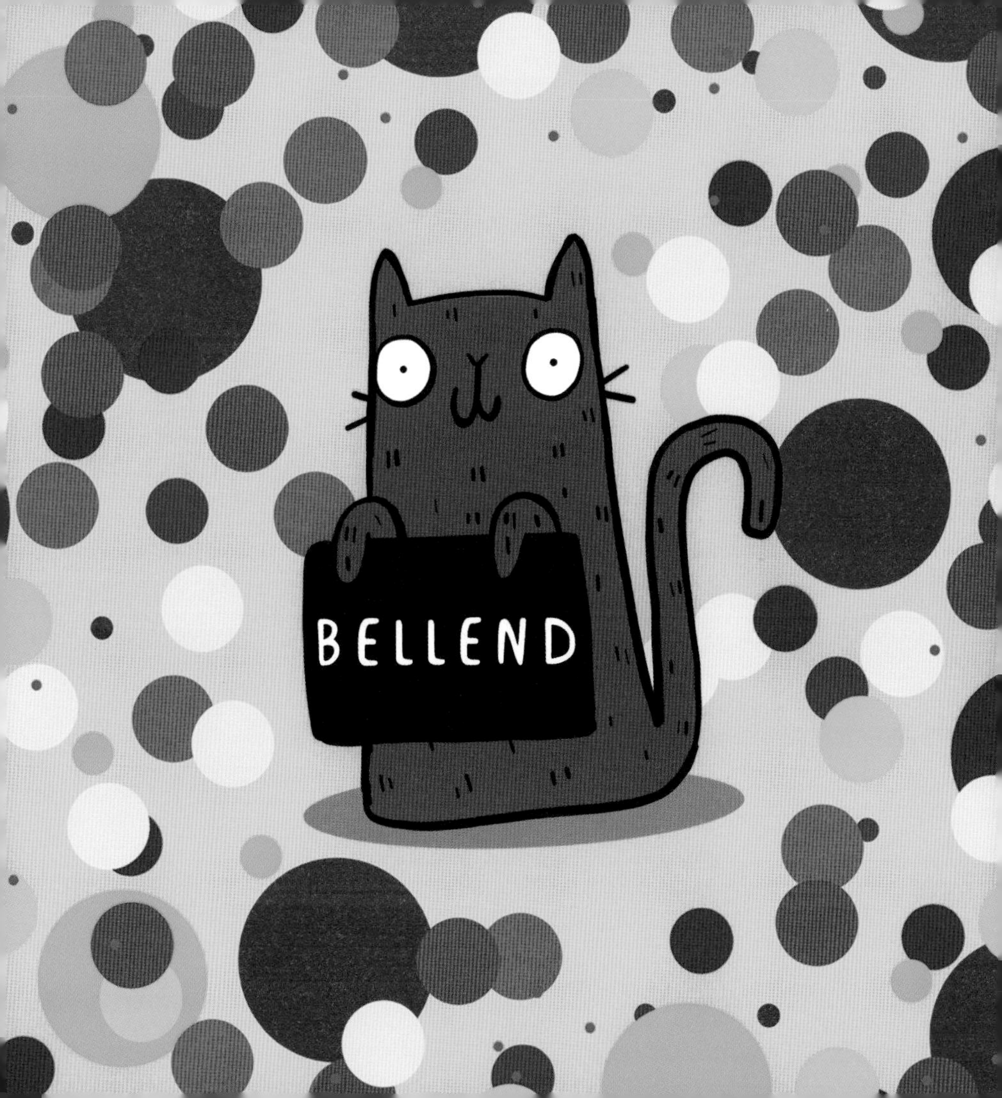
BELLEND

EVERYTHING SUCKS.
EAT SOME BISCUITS.

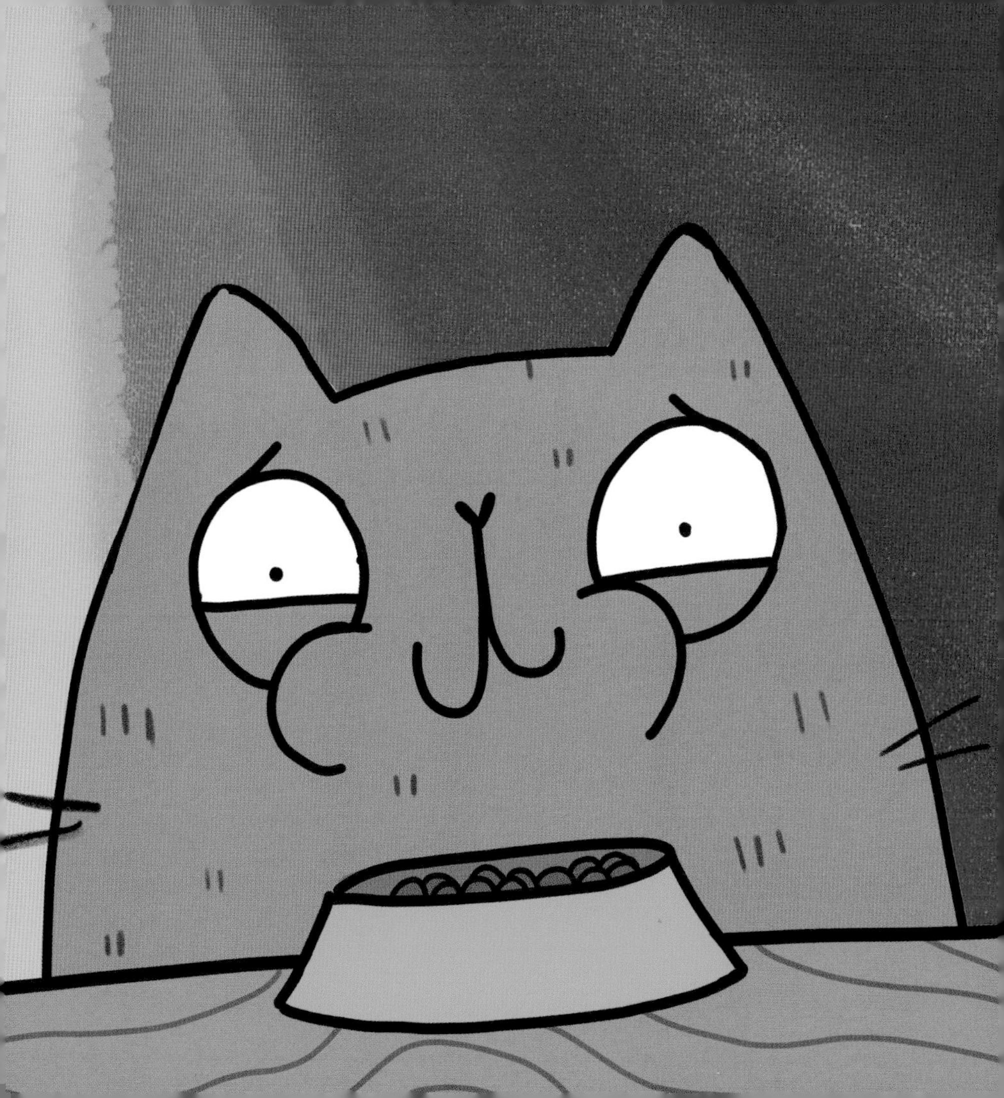

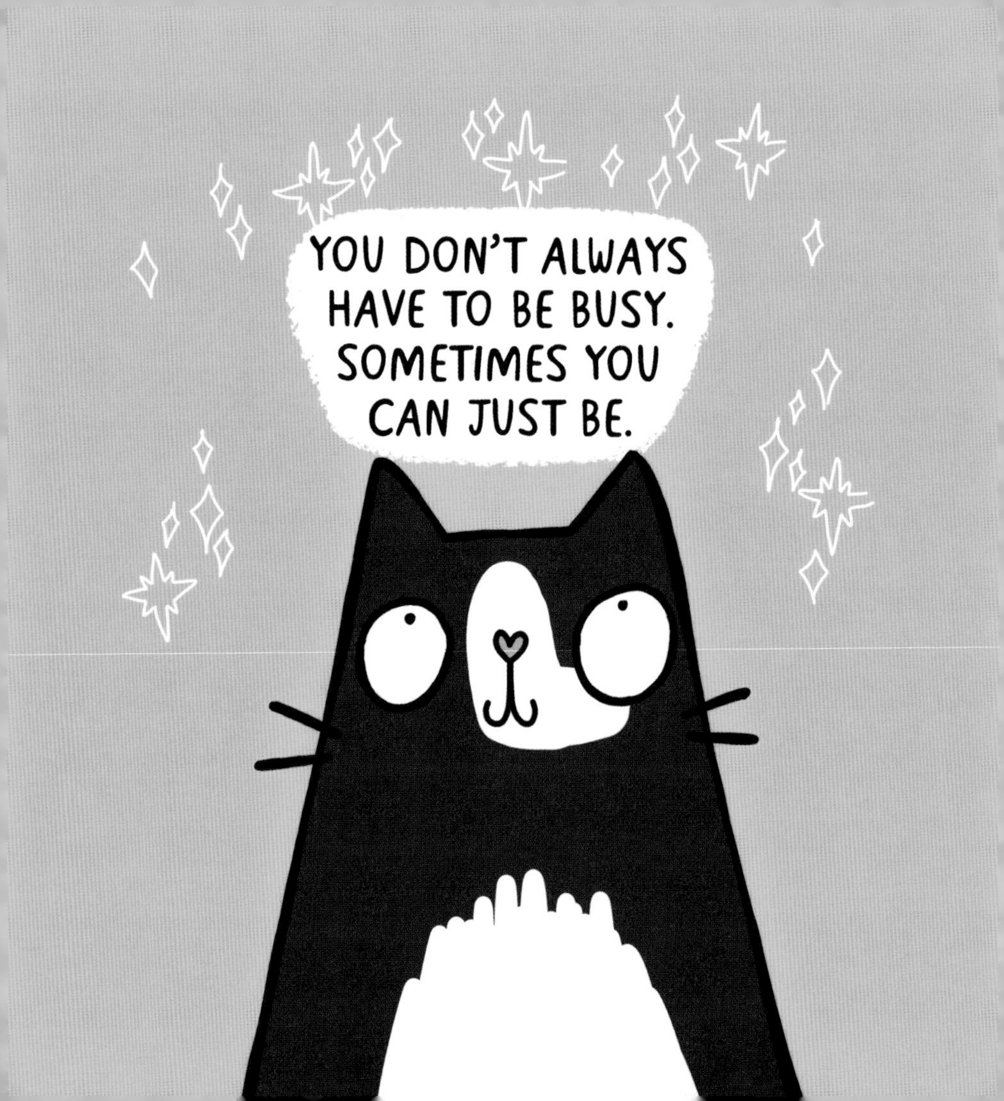
YOU DON'T ALWAYS HAVE TO BE BUSY. SOMETIMES YOU CAN JUST BE.

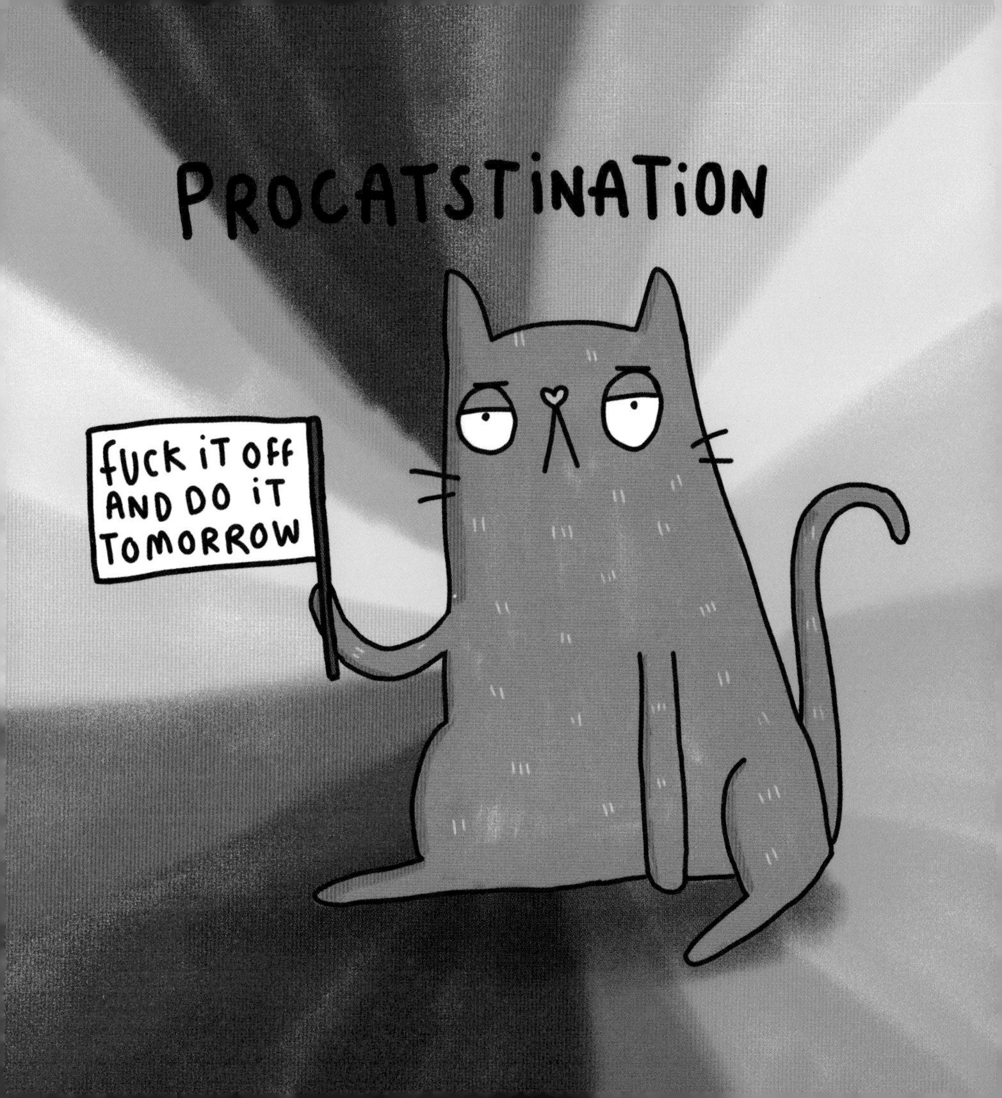
PROCATSTINATION
FUCK IT OFF AND DO IT TOMORROW

COMFORT ZONES ARE COSY.
STAY IN YOURS AS LONG
AS YOU NEED TO.

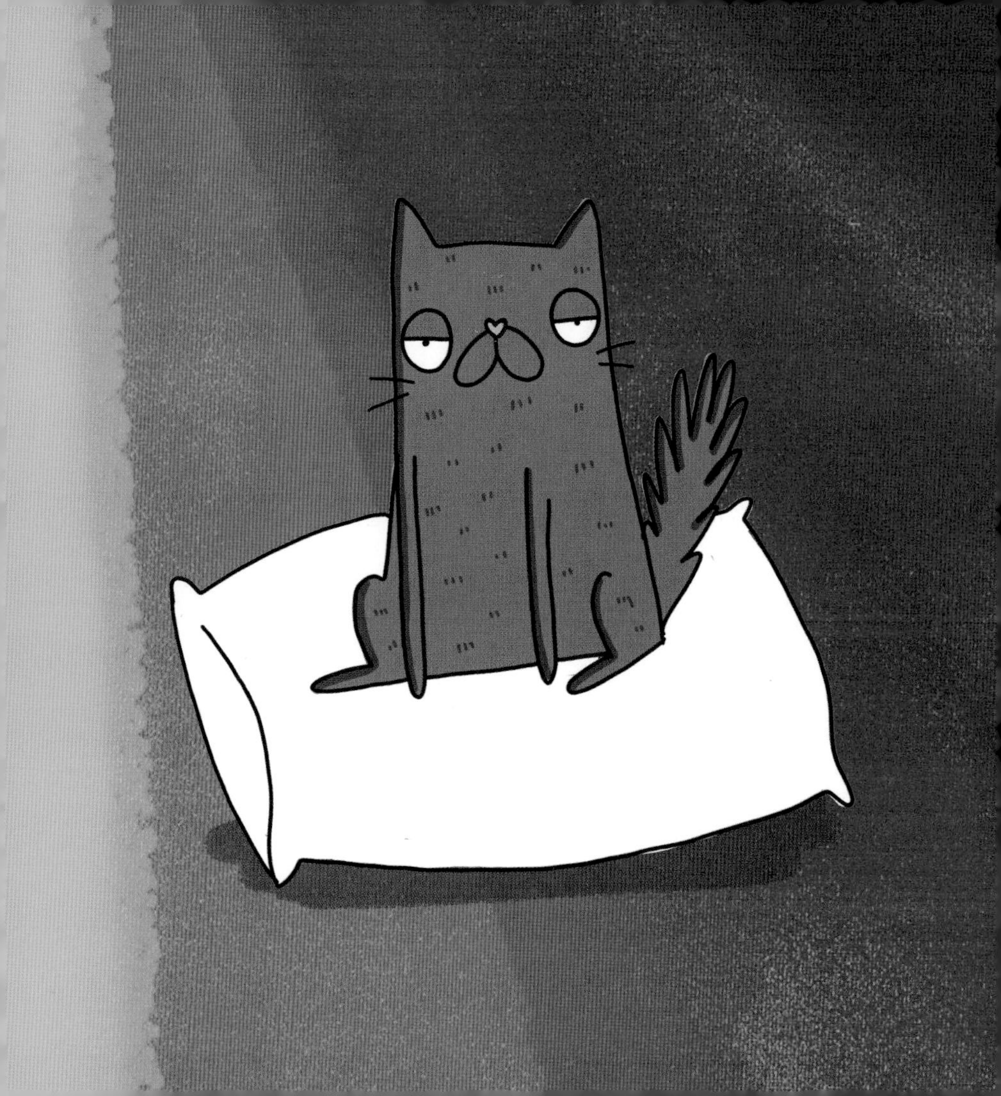

STOP OVERWORKING, YOU SILLY BITCH

CORPURRATE CAT

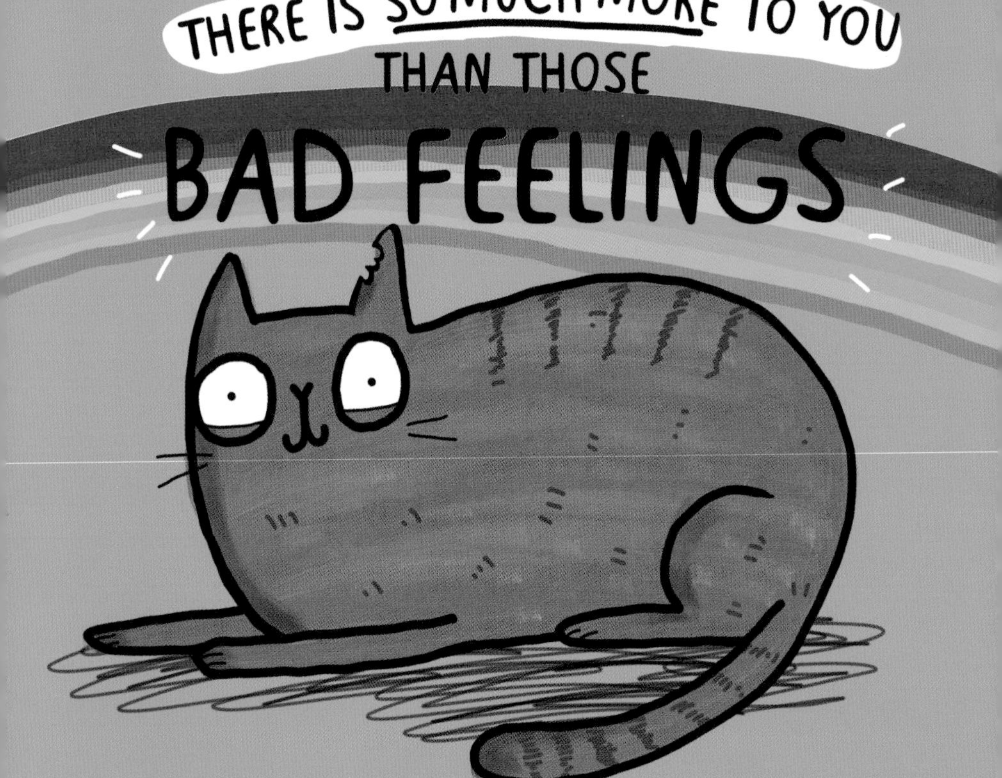
THERE IS SO MUCH MORE TO YOU
THAN THOSE
BAD FEELINGS

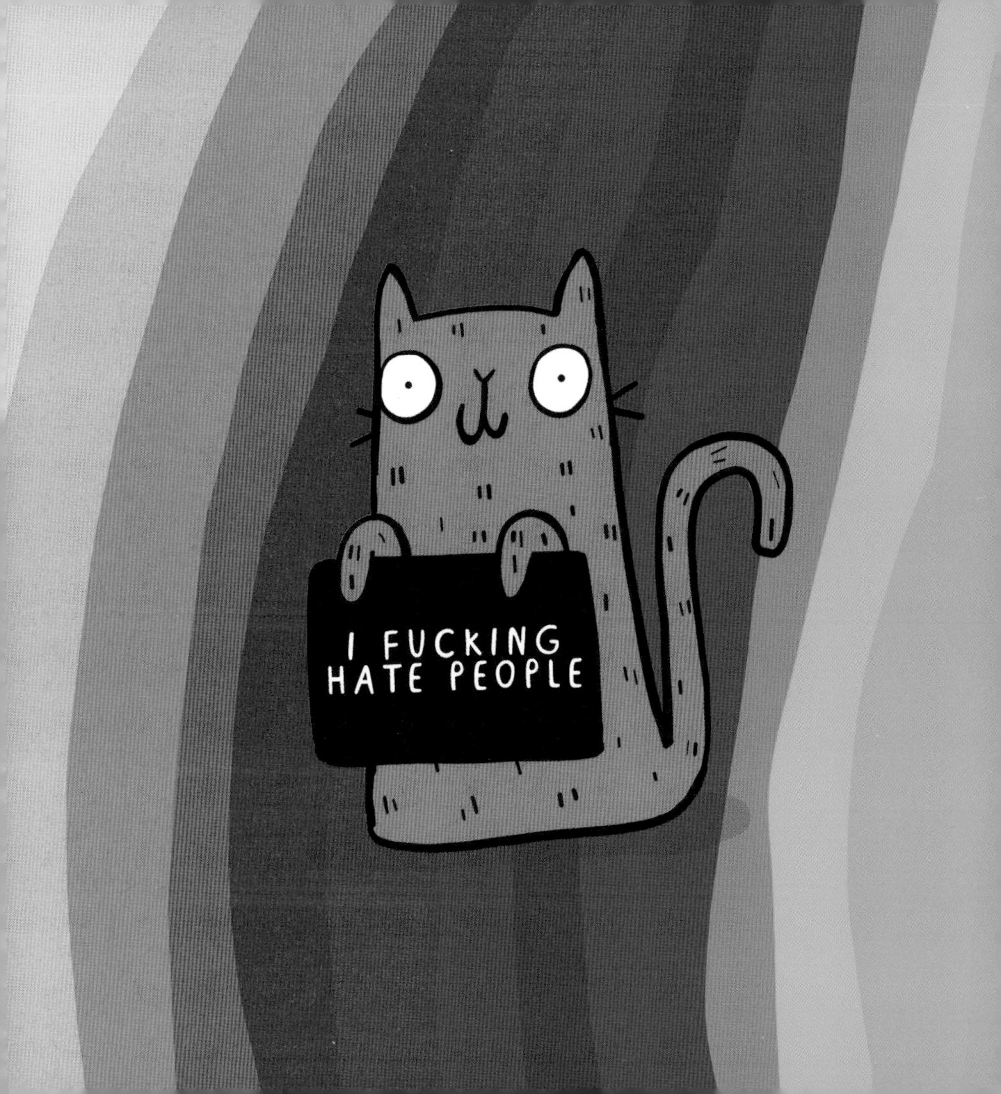
I FUCKING
HATE PEOPLE

GIVE ME SOME SPACE

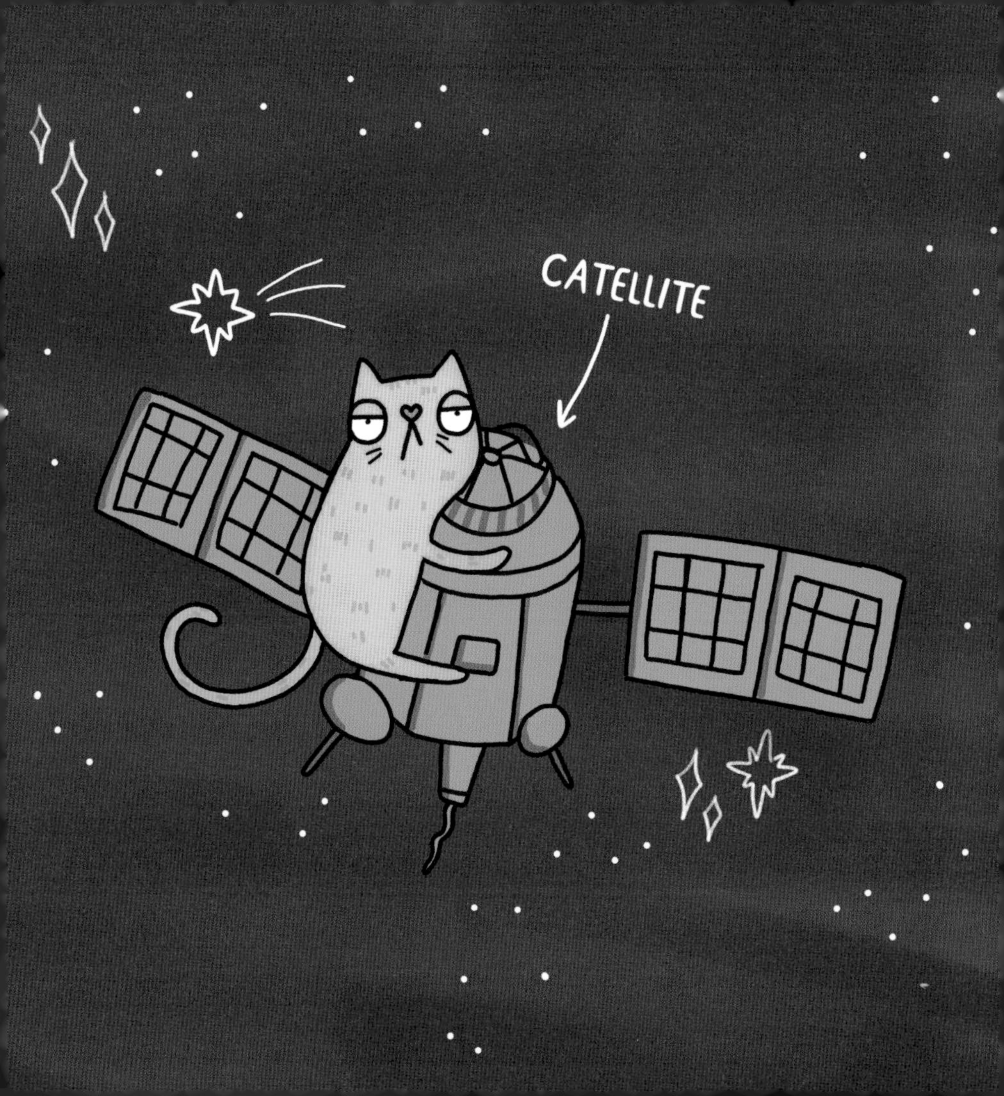
CATELLITE

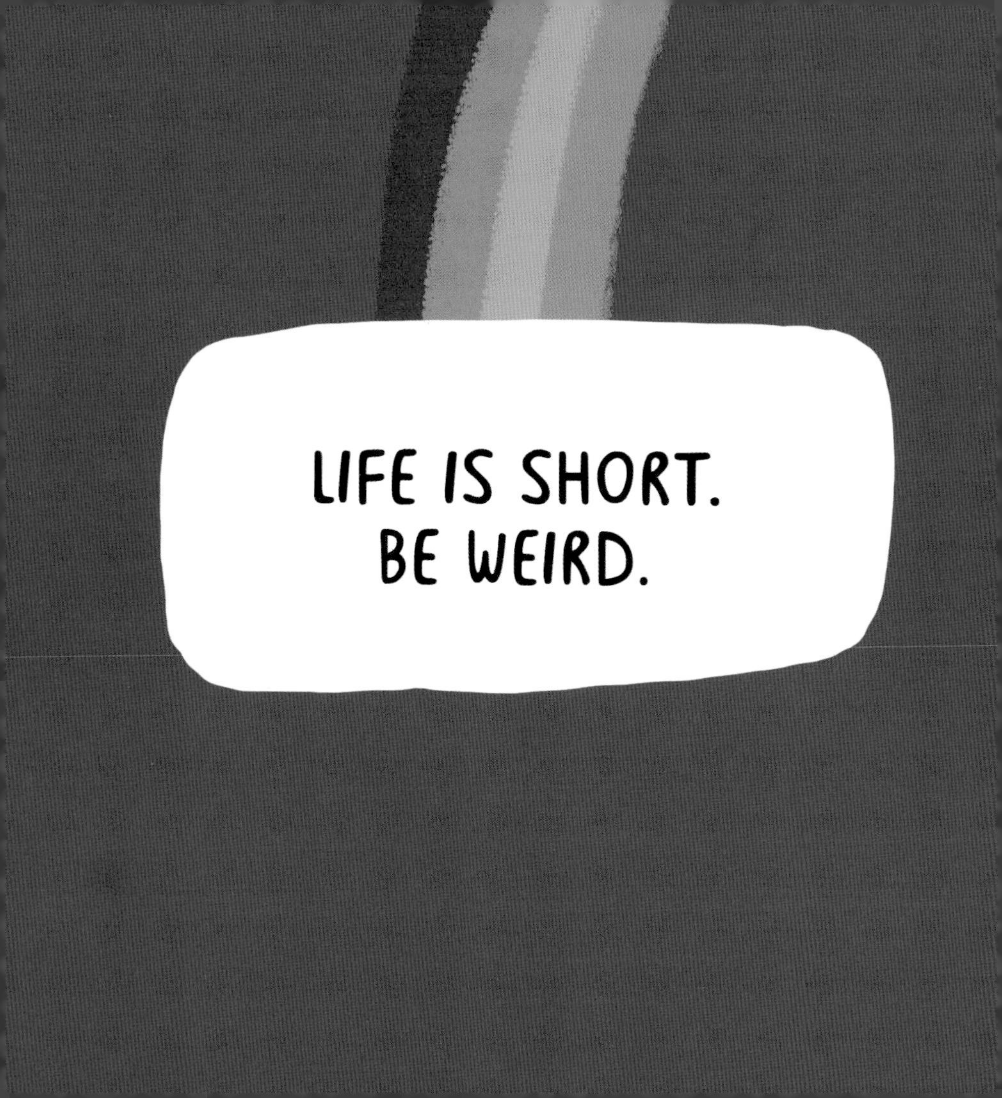
LIFE IS SHORT.
BE WEIRD.

CATXOLOTL

YOU CAN CARE ABOUT PEOPLE ...

WITHOUT HAVING TO CARRY
THEIR SHIT AROUND WITH YOU

I AM NO LONGER AVAILABLE
FOR YOUR BULLSHIT

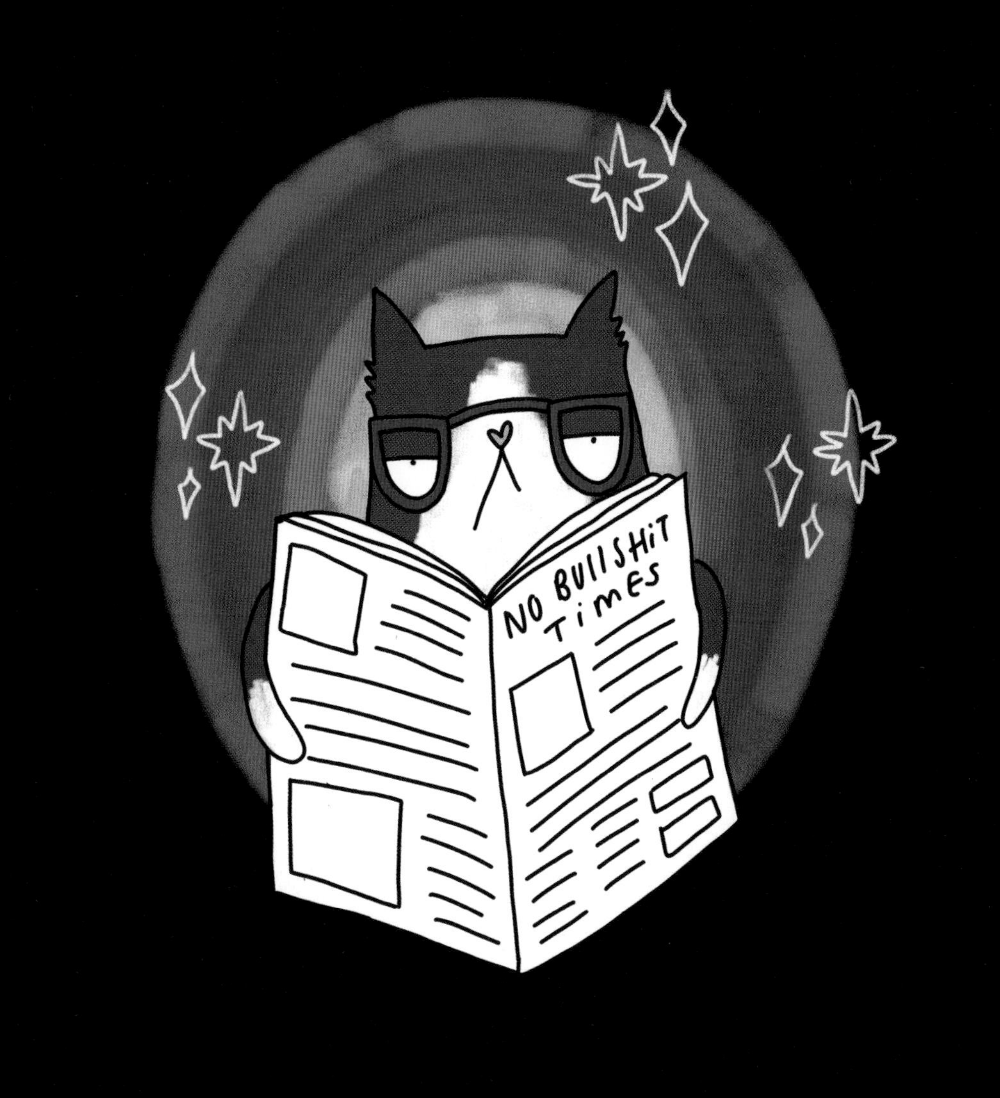
NO BULLSHIT
TIMES

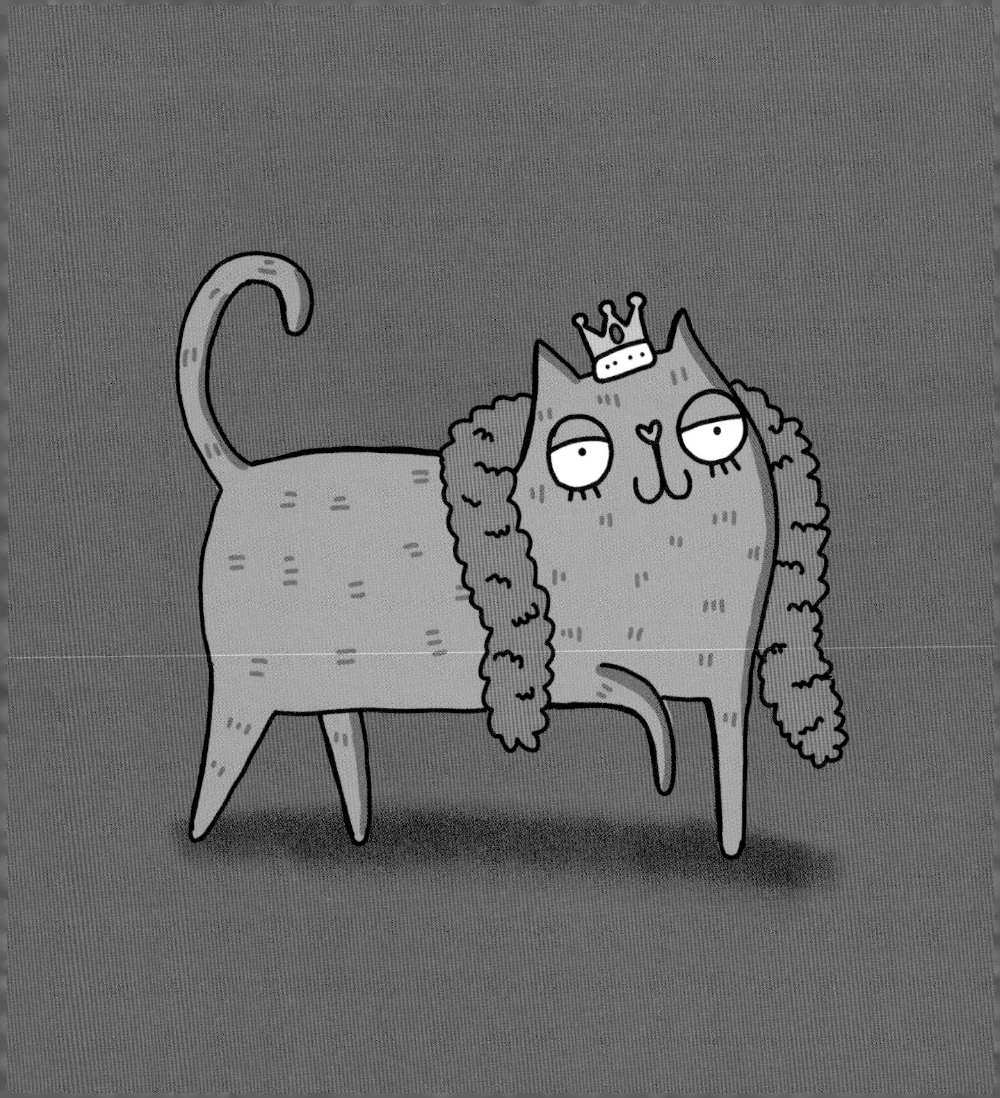

DON'T FORGET THAT YOU'RE A QUEEN

MARVEL AT YOUR
MOTHERFUCKING
RESILIENCE

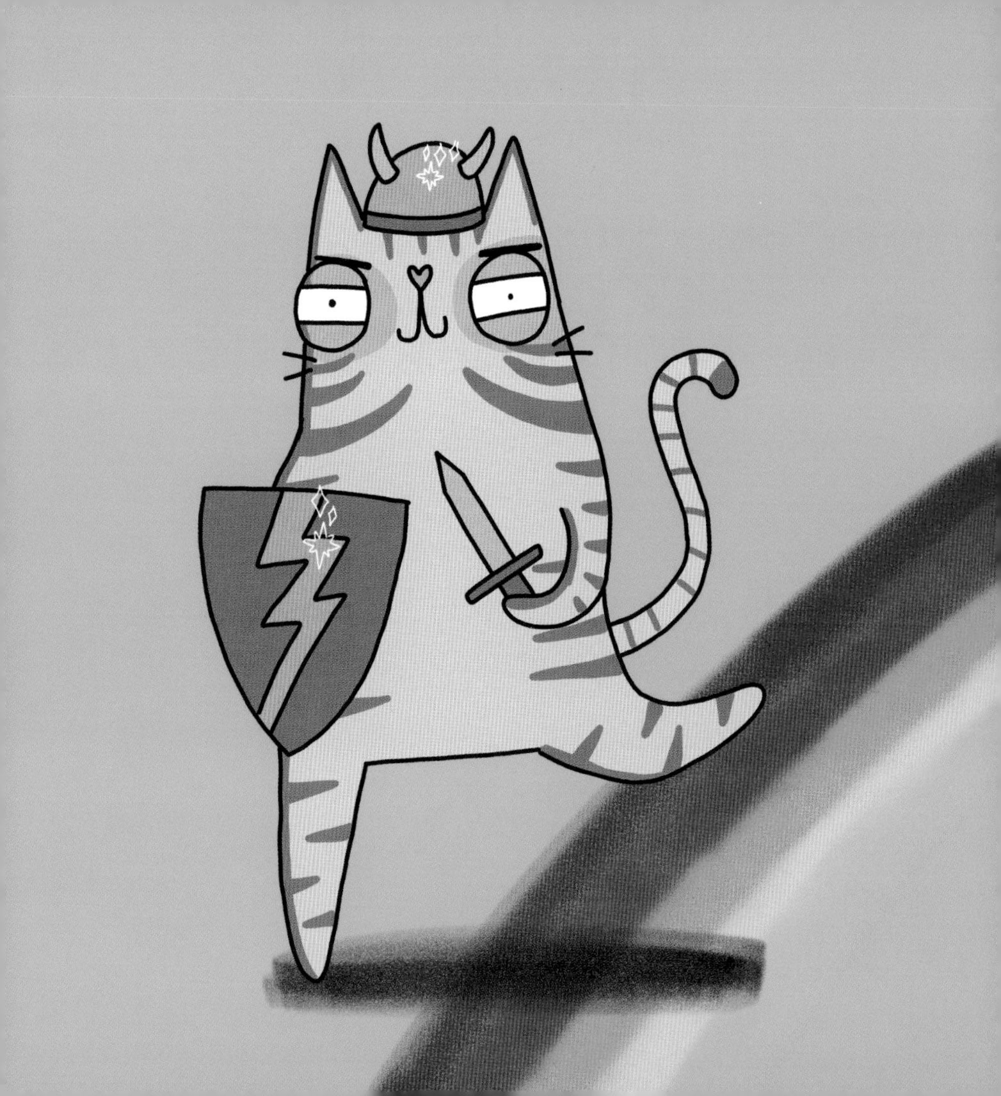

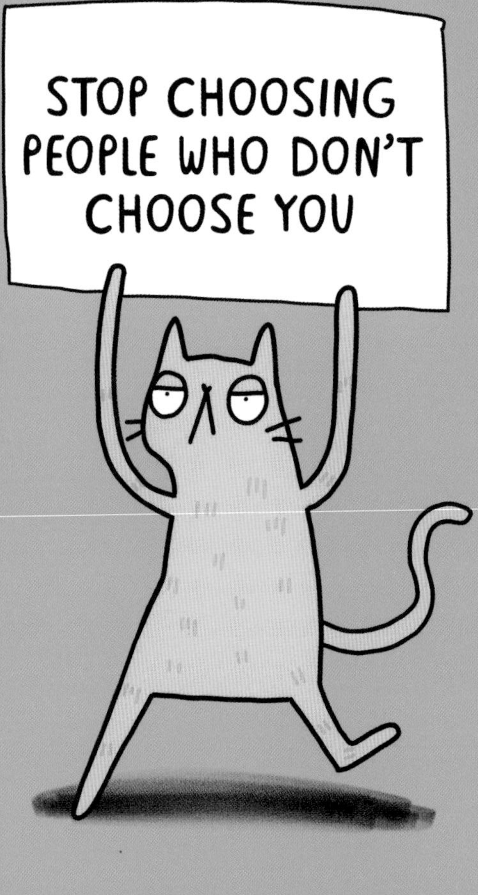
STOP CHOOSING PEOPLE WHO DON'T CHOOSE YOU

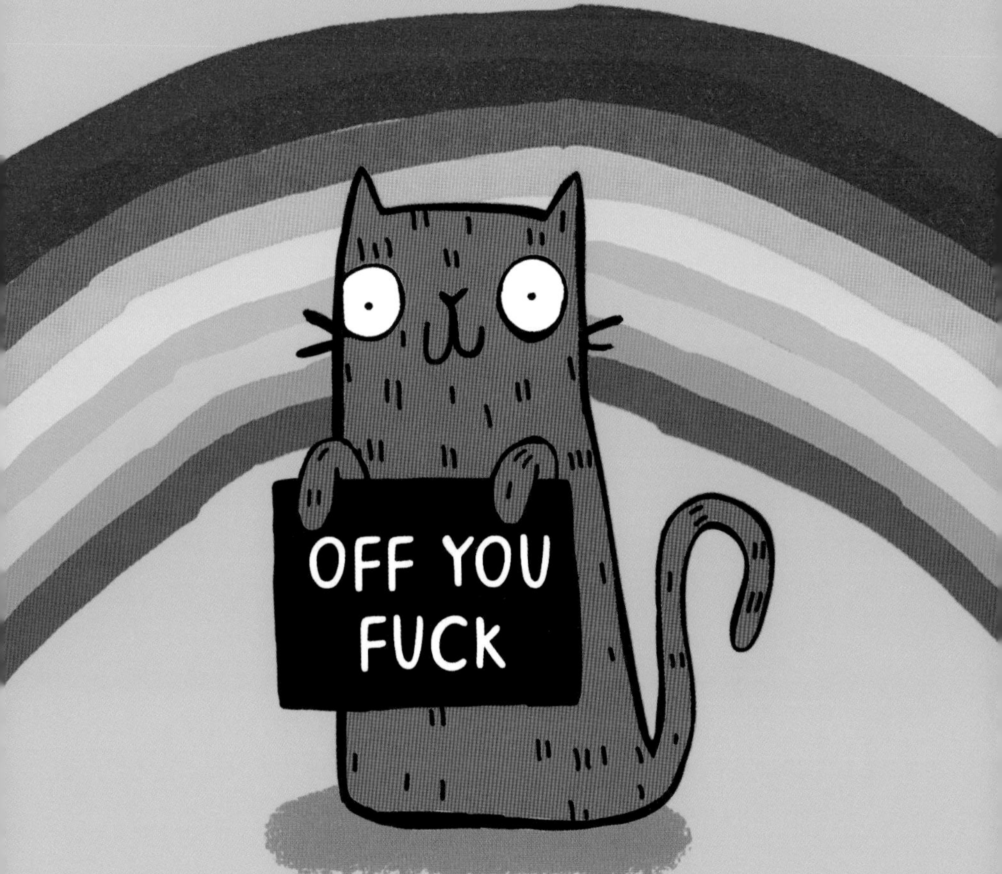
OFF YOU
FUCK

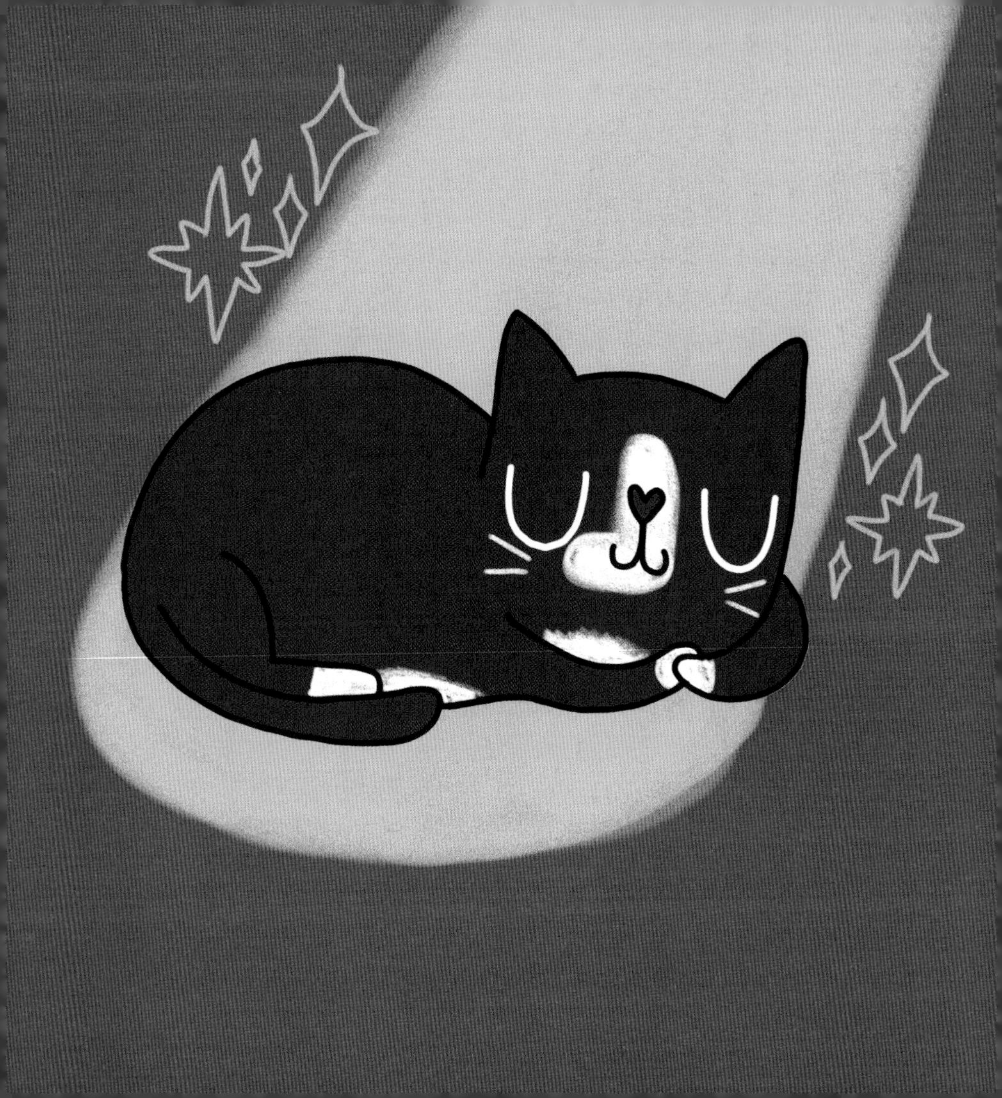

FORGET THE WANKERS AND
SOAK UP SOME SUNSHINE

IF THEY HURT YOU
THEY CAN GET IN THE SEA

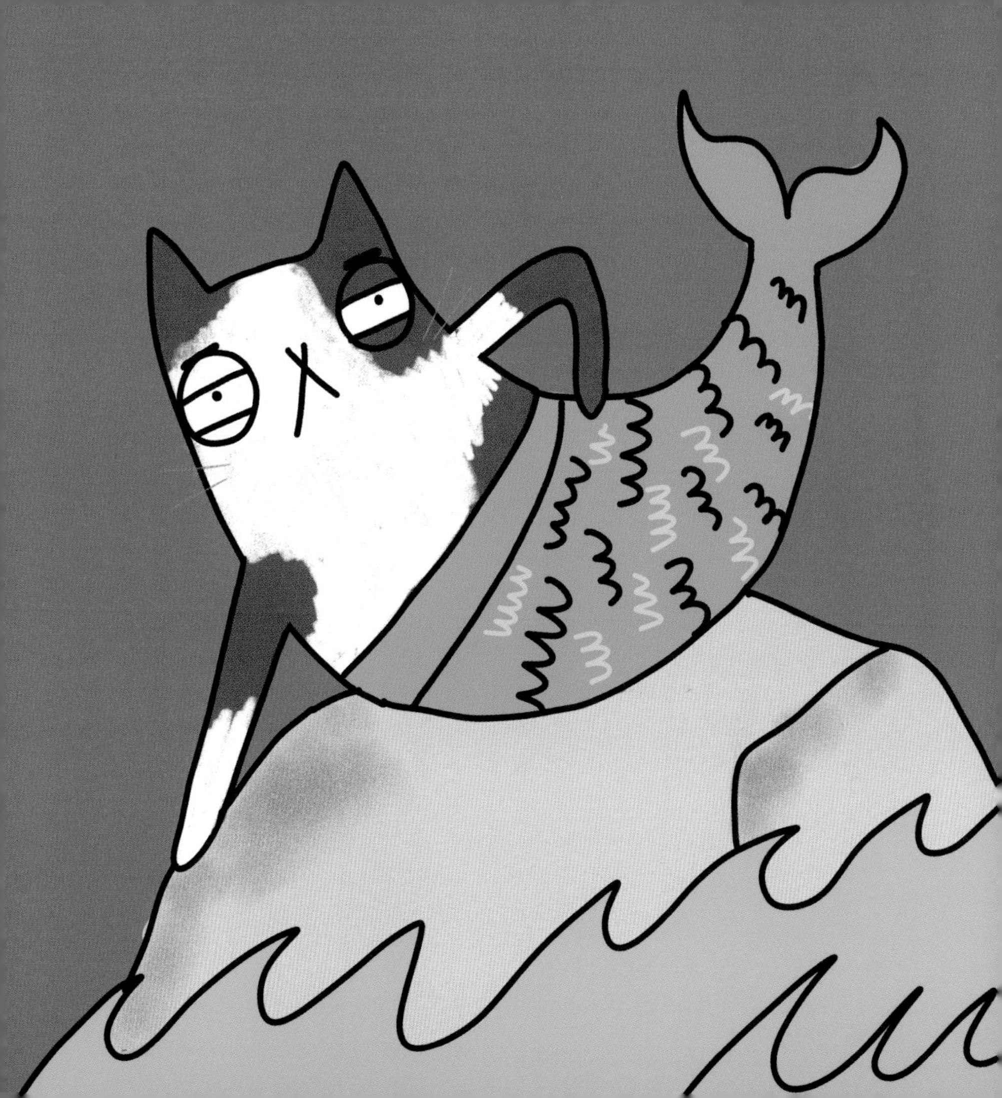

BE PURROUD
OF WHO YOU ARE

STAND UP FUR YOURSELF.
DON'T LET PEOPLE
WALK ALL OVER YOU.

YOU ARE DOING A BRILLIANT
JOB AND YOU ARE LOVED.
(NOW FEED ME.)

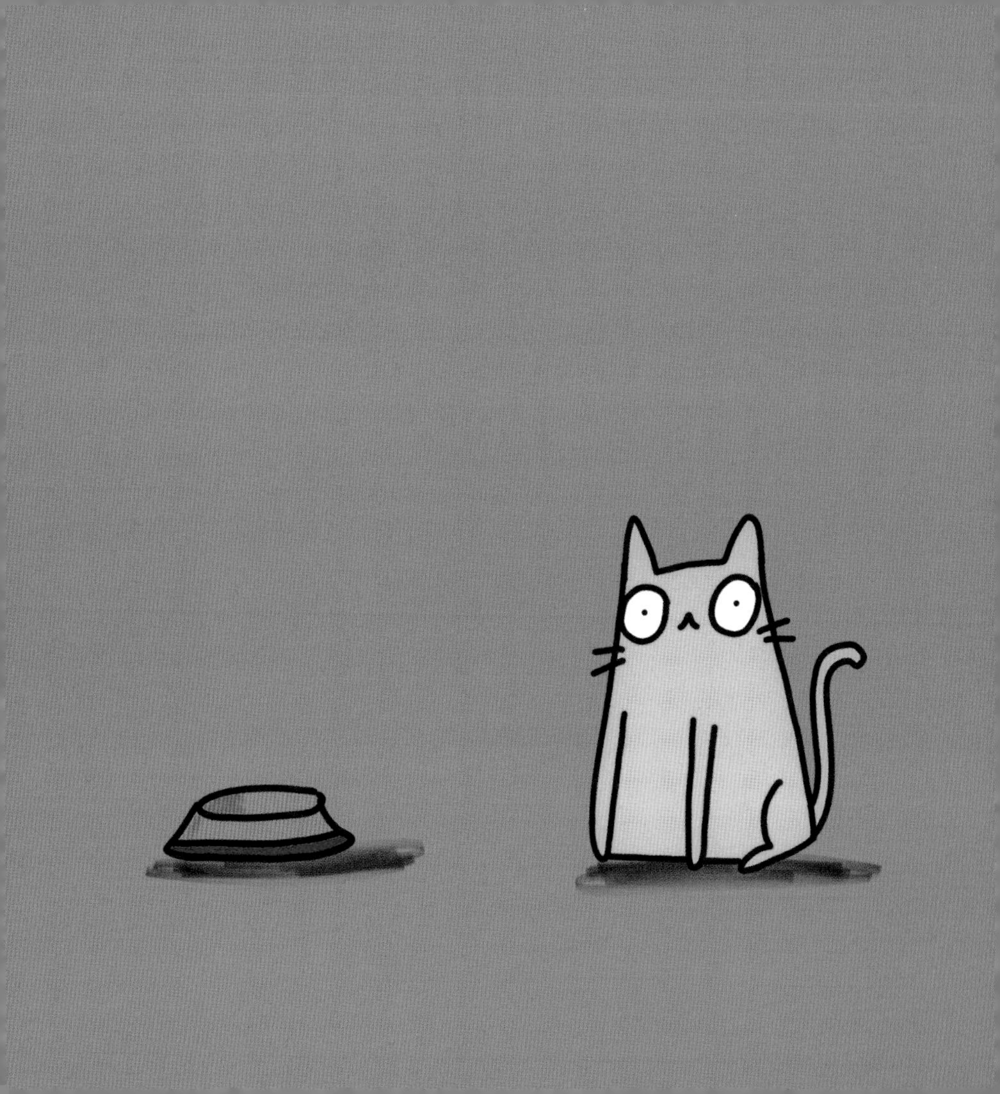

IT DOESN'T MATTER IF YOU'RE
A MESS AS LONG AS YOU'RE
HAVING FUN

ONE DAY SOON
EVERYTHING WILL BE
A BIT LESS CRAP.
UNTIL THEN
HAVE A NAP.

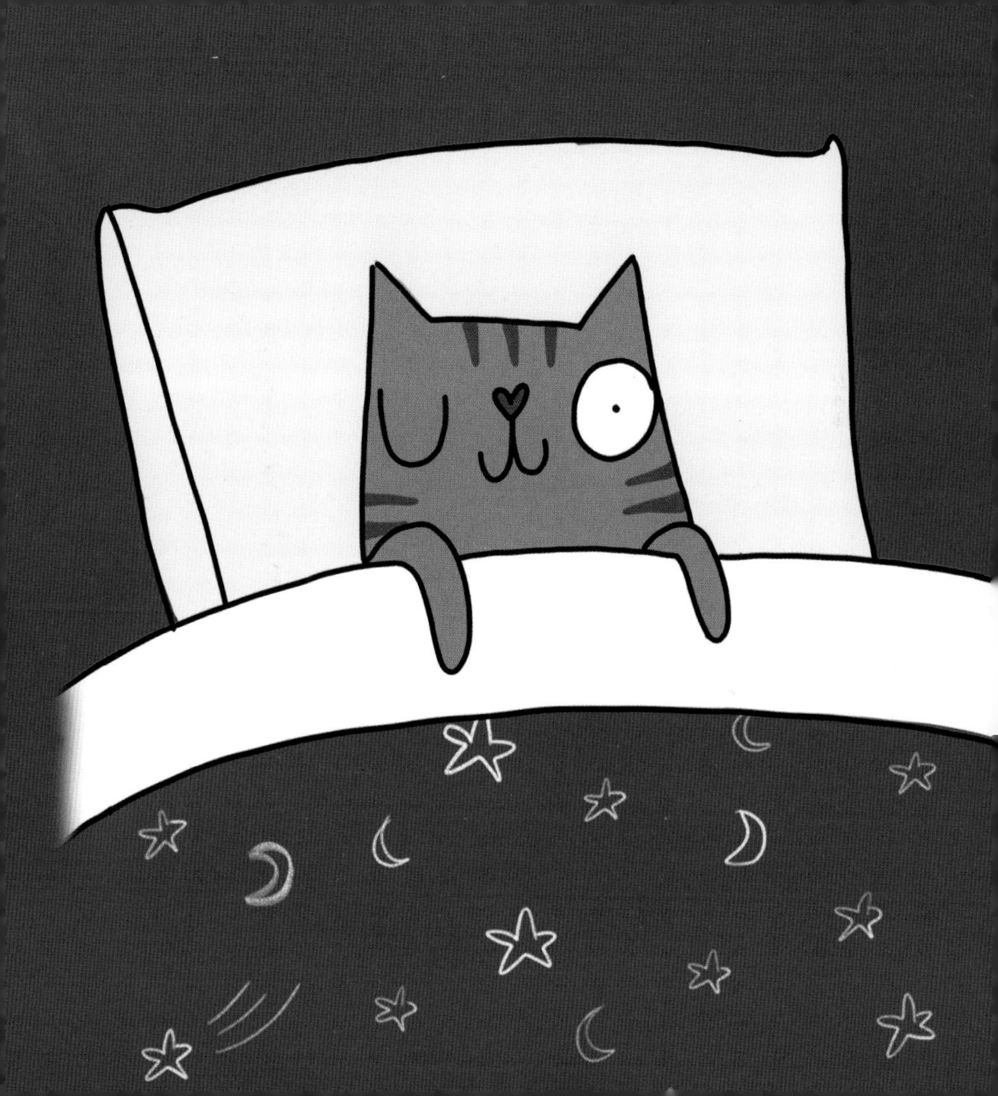

FOCUS ON THE MAGIC THINGS

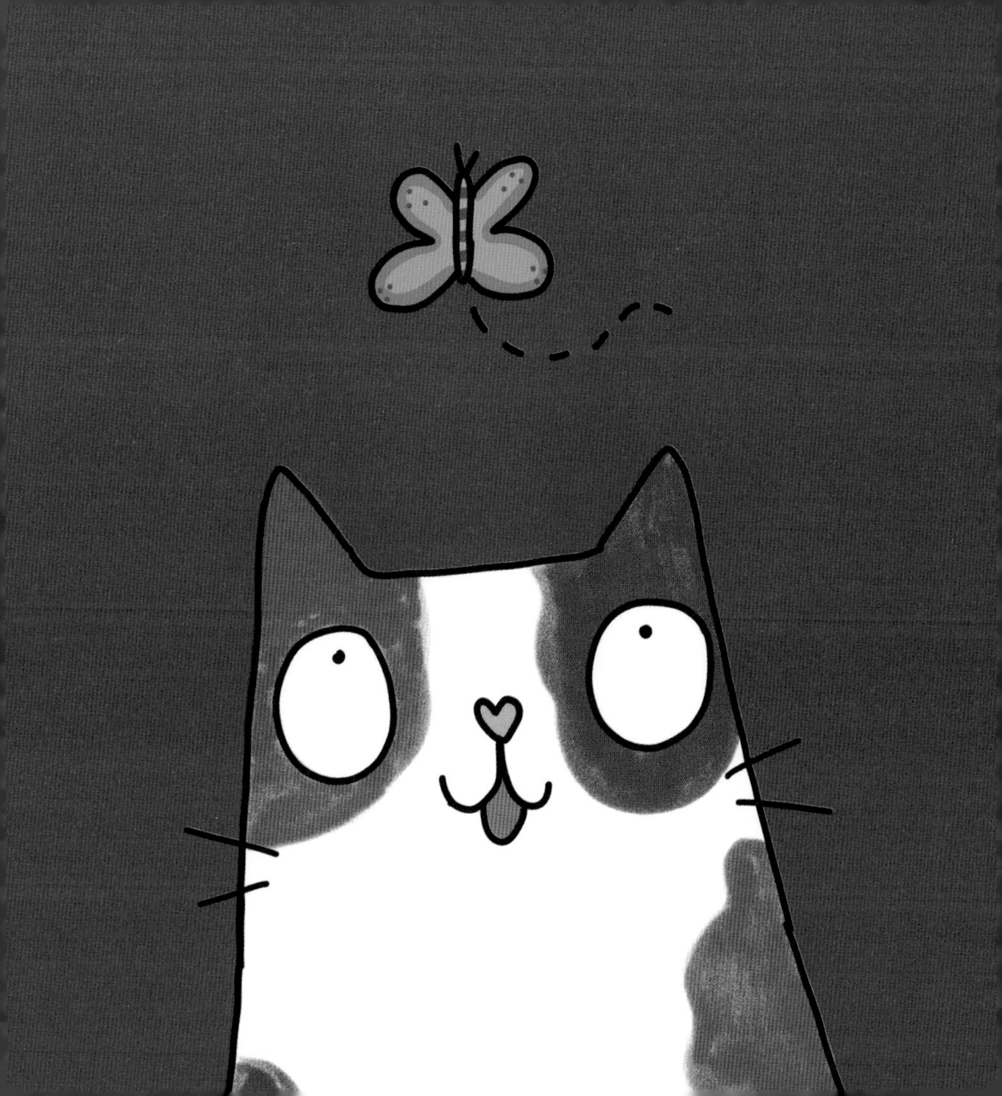

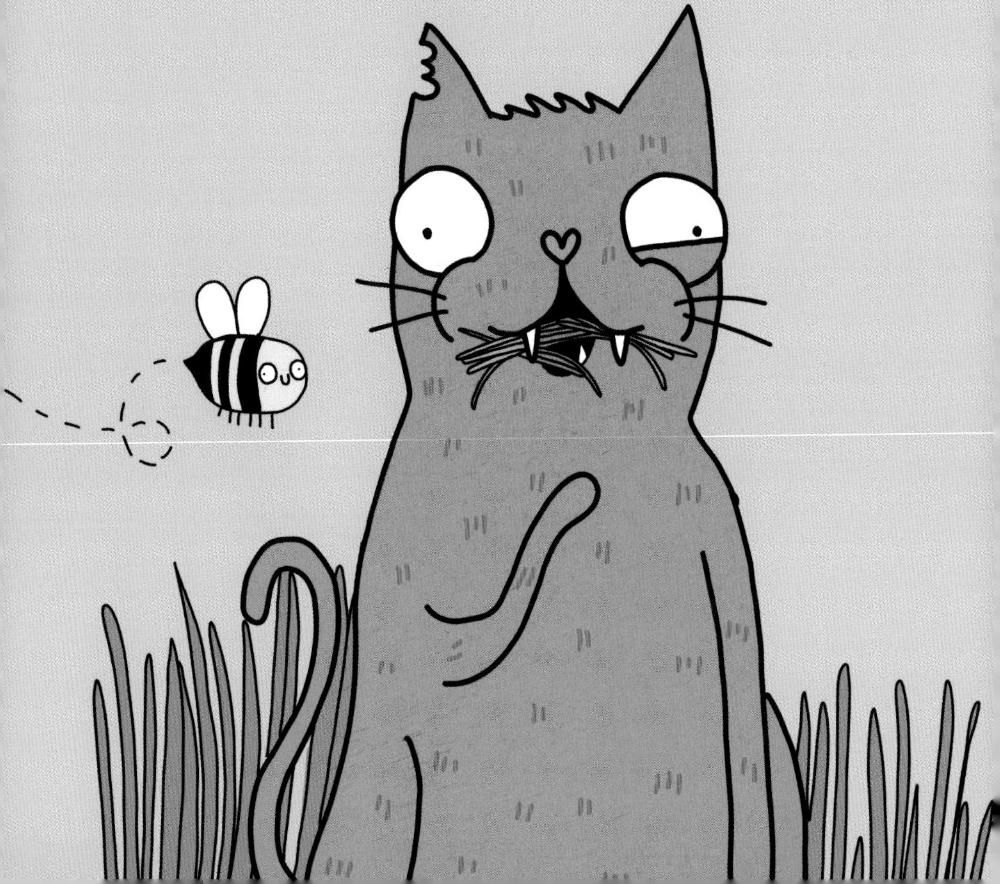

THERE IS MORE TO EXPLORE
OUTSIDE YOUR DOOR

JUST DO IT

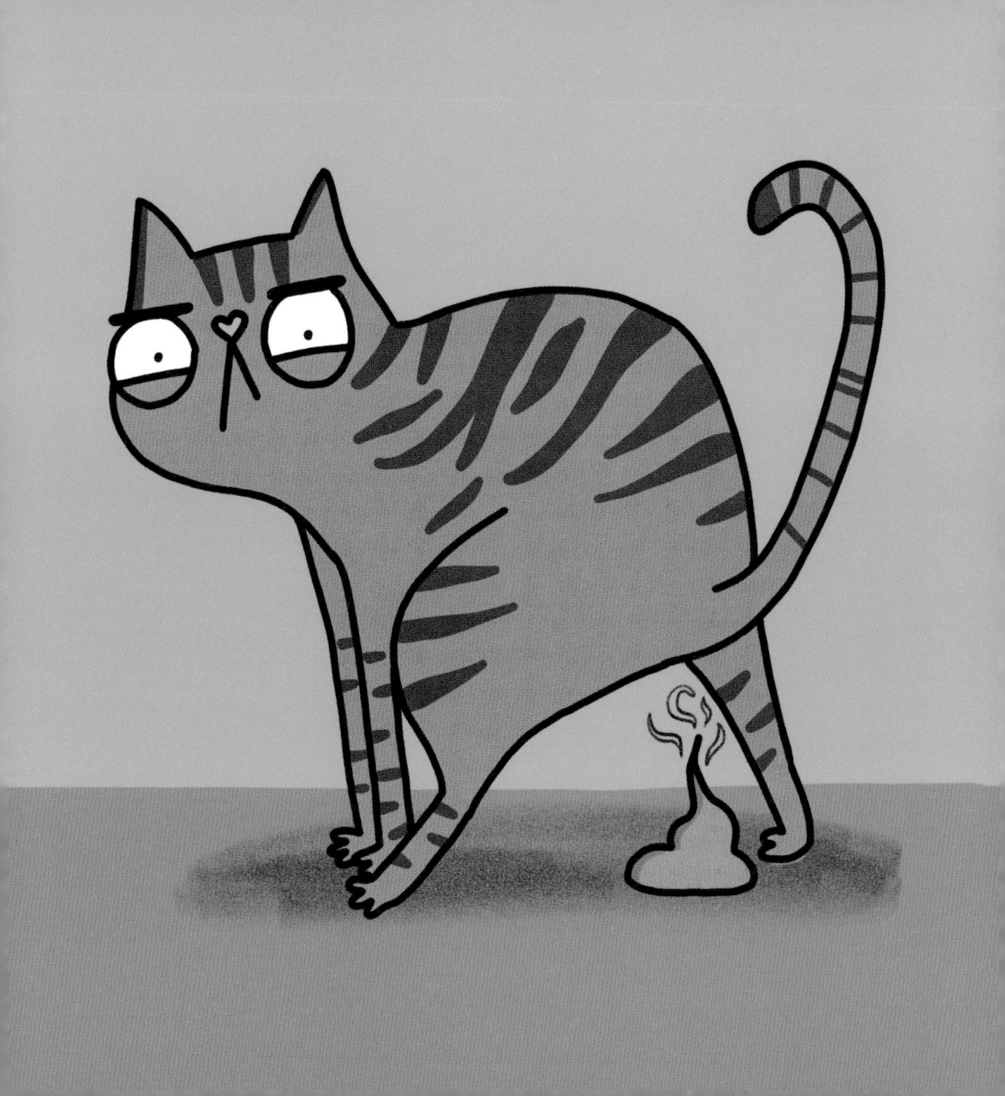

SOMETIMES WHEN YOU GET A
NEW PURRSPECTIVE, THINGS
APPEAR LESS SCARY

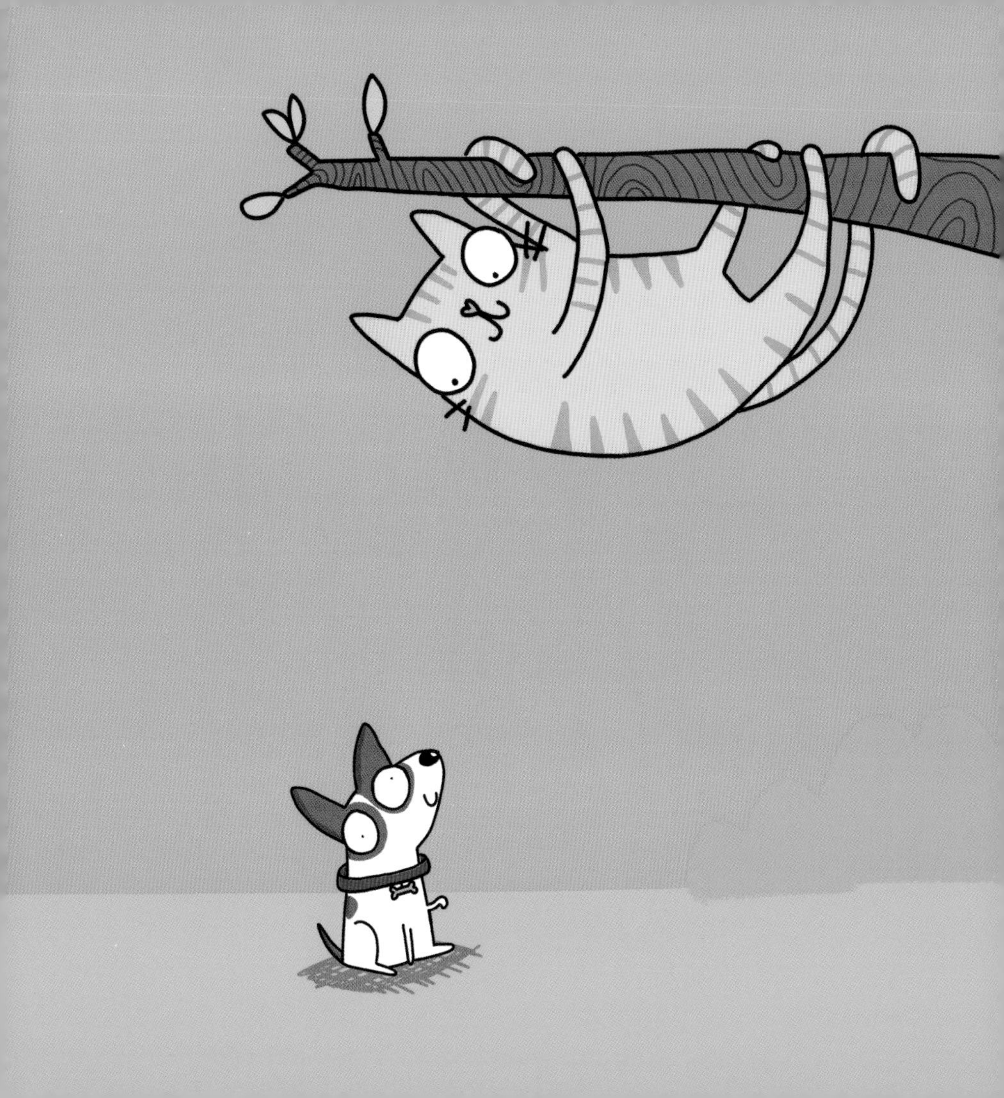

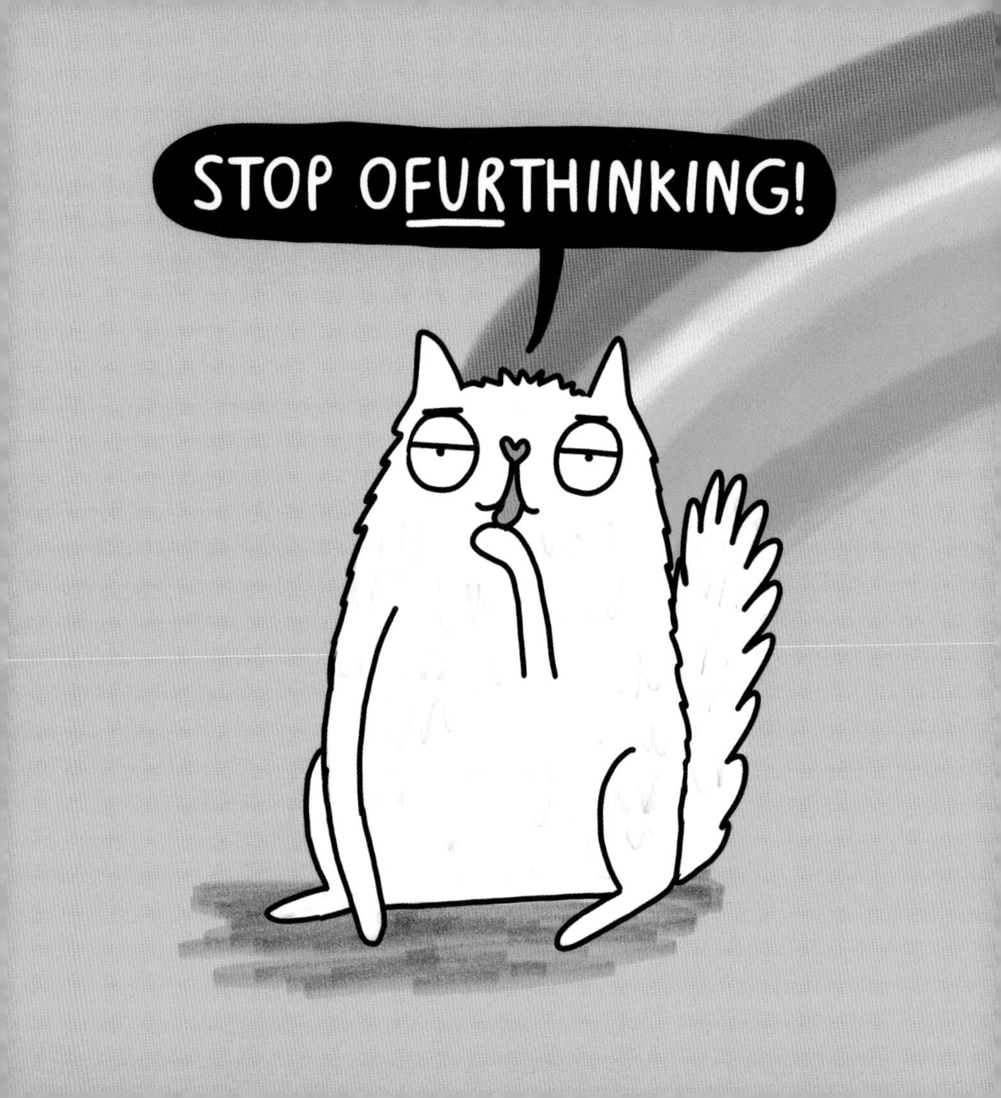
STOP OFURTHINKING!

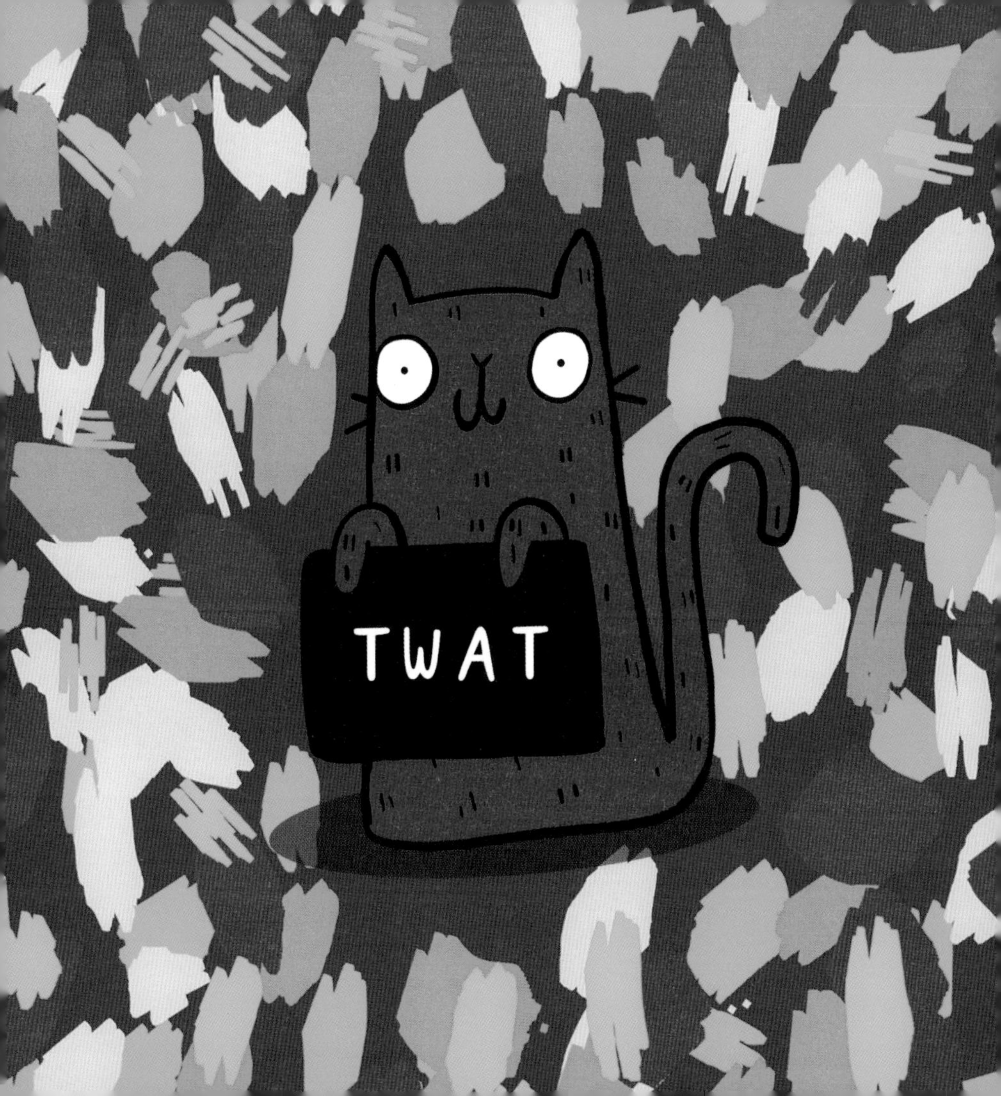
TWAT

DON'T LET YESTERDAY TAKE UP
TOO MUCH OF TODAY

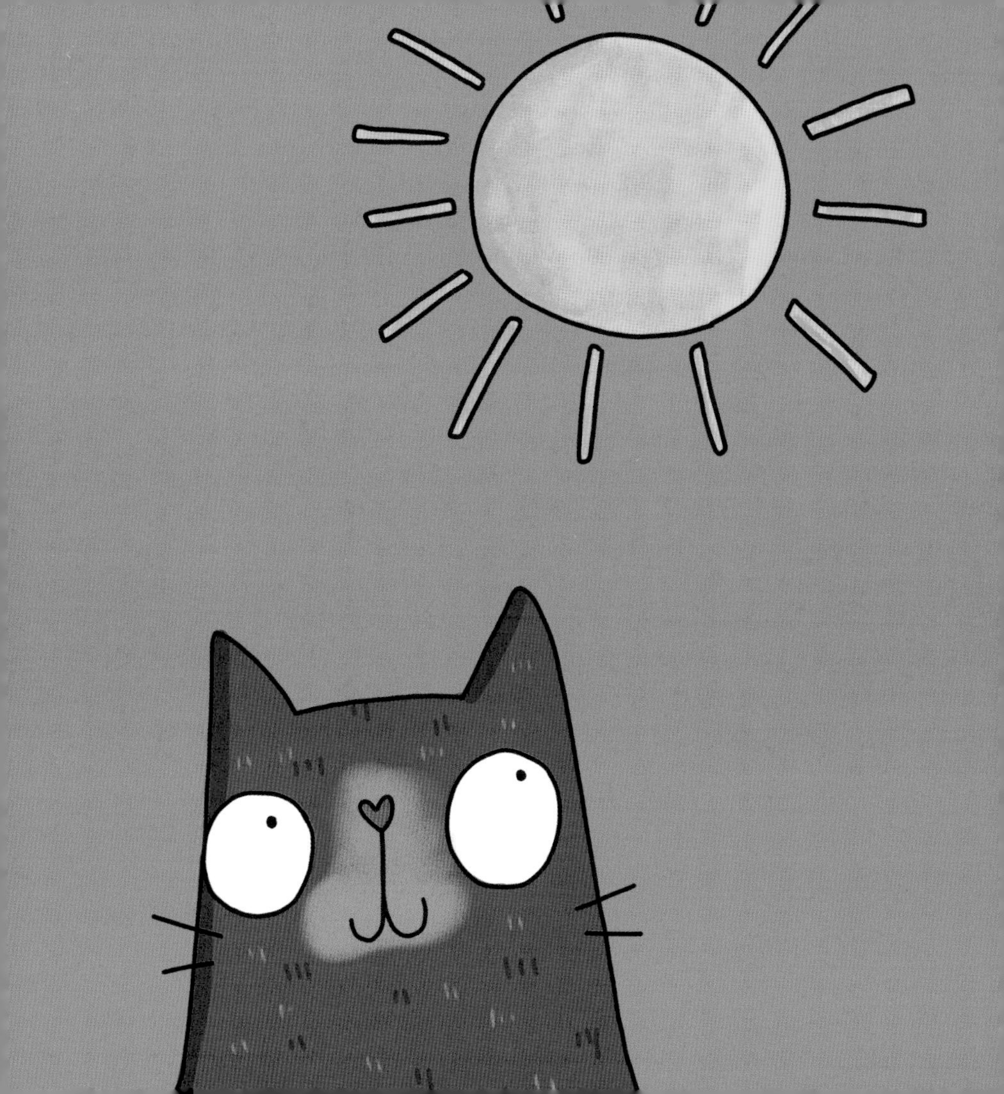

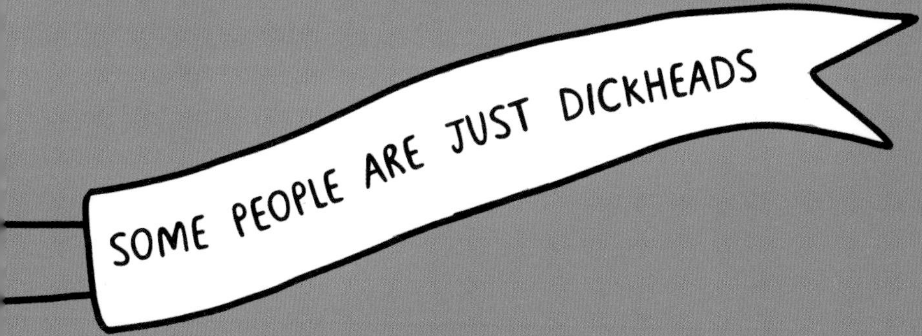
SOME PEOPLE ARE JUST DICKHEADS

IF THEY DON'T LIKE YOU THEN...

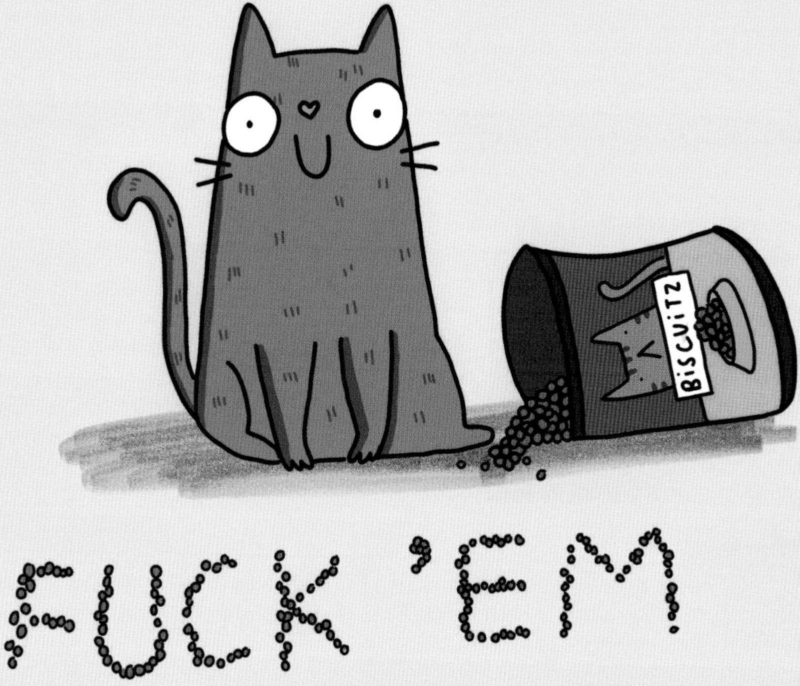
BISCUITZ
FUCK 'EM

REMEMBER HOW
MAGIC YOU ARE,
BITCH

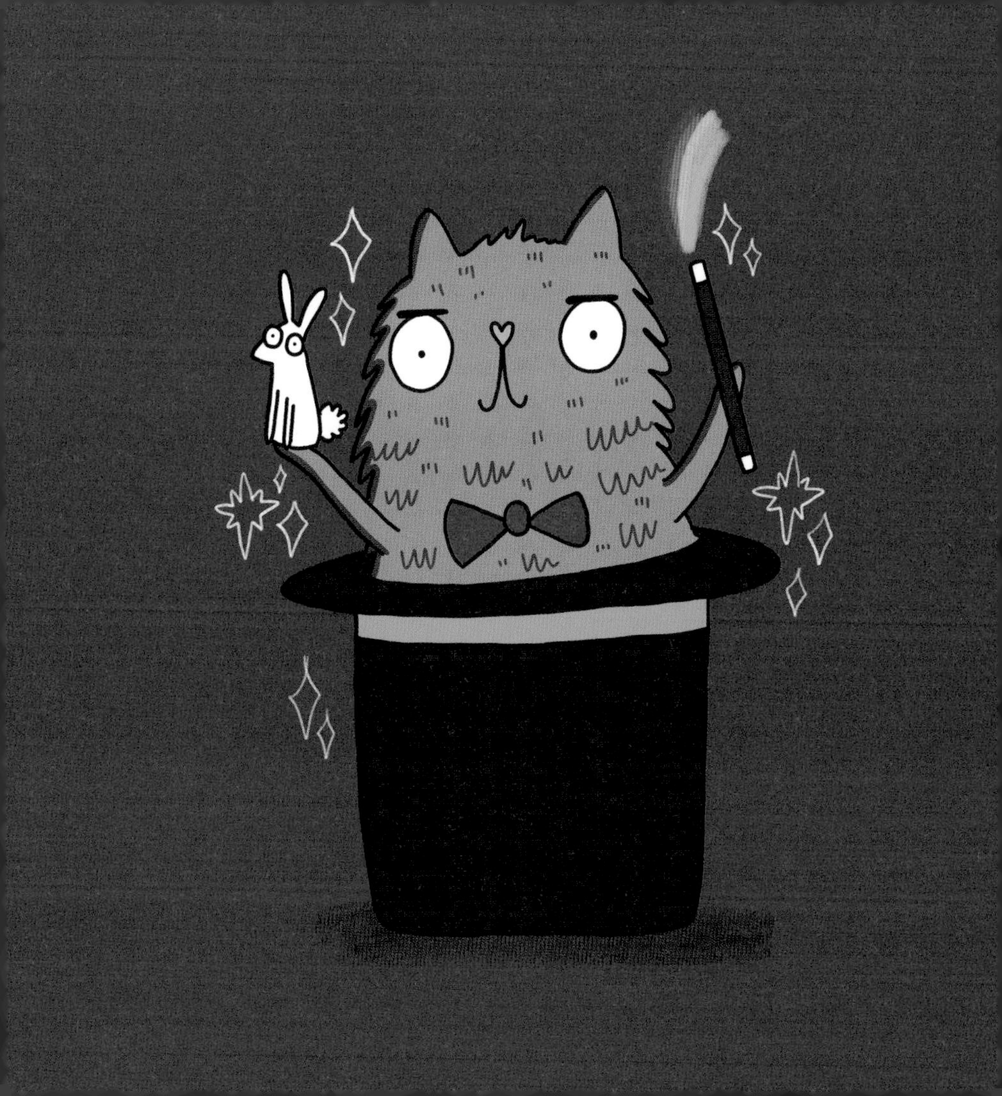

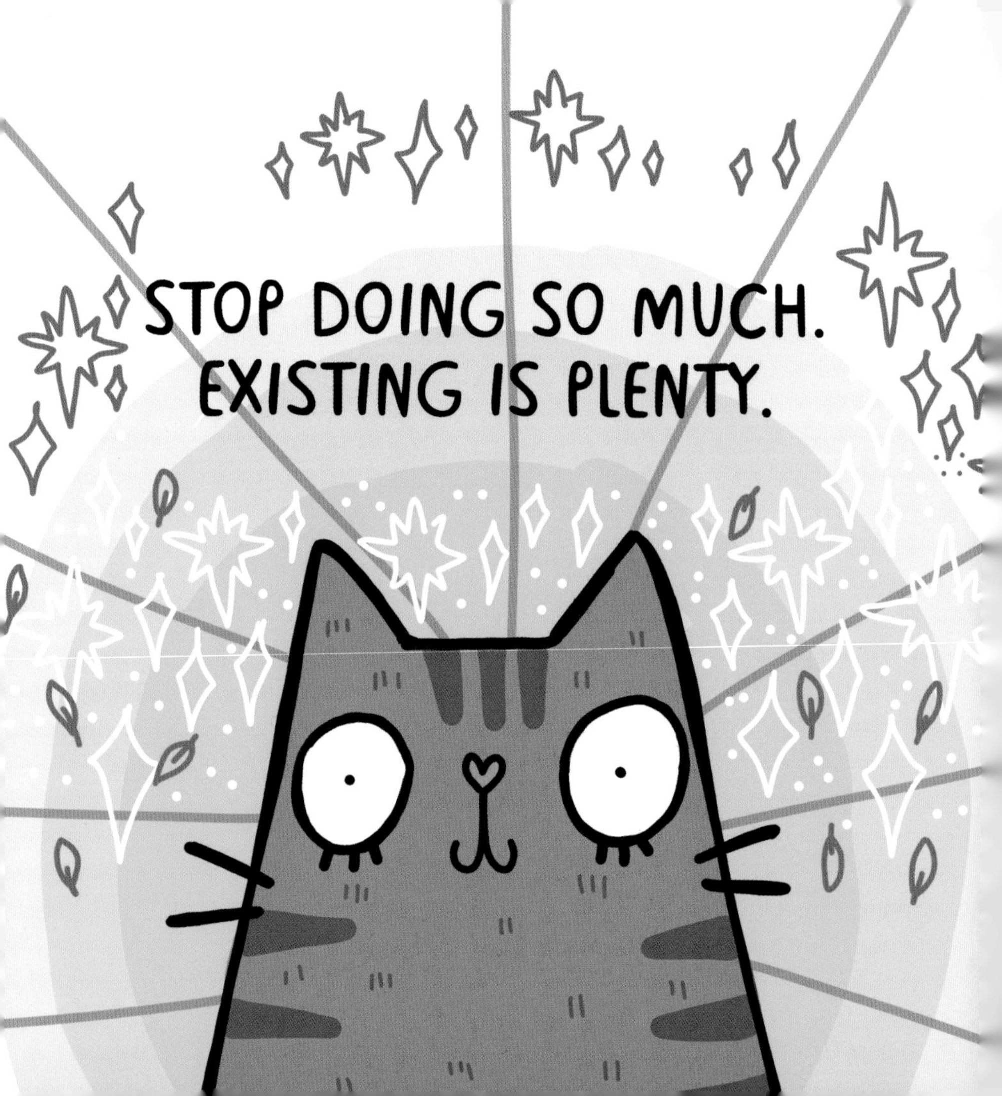
STOP DOING SO MUCH.
EXISTING IS PLENTY.

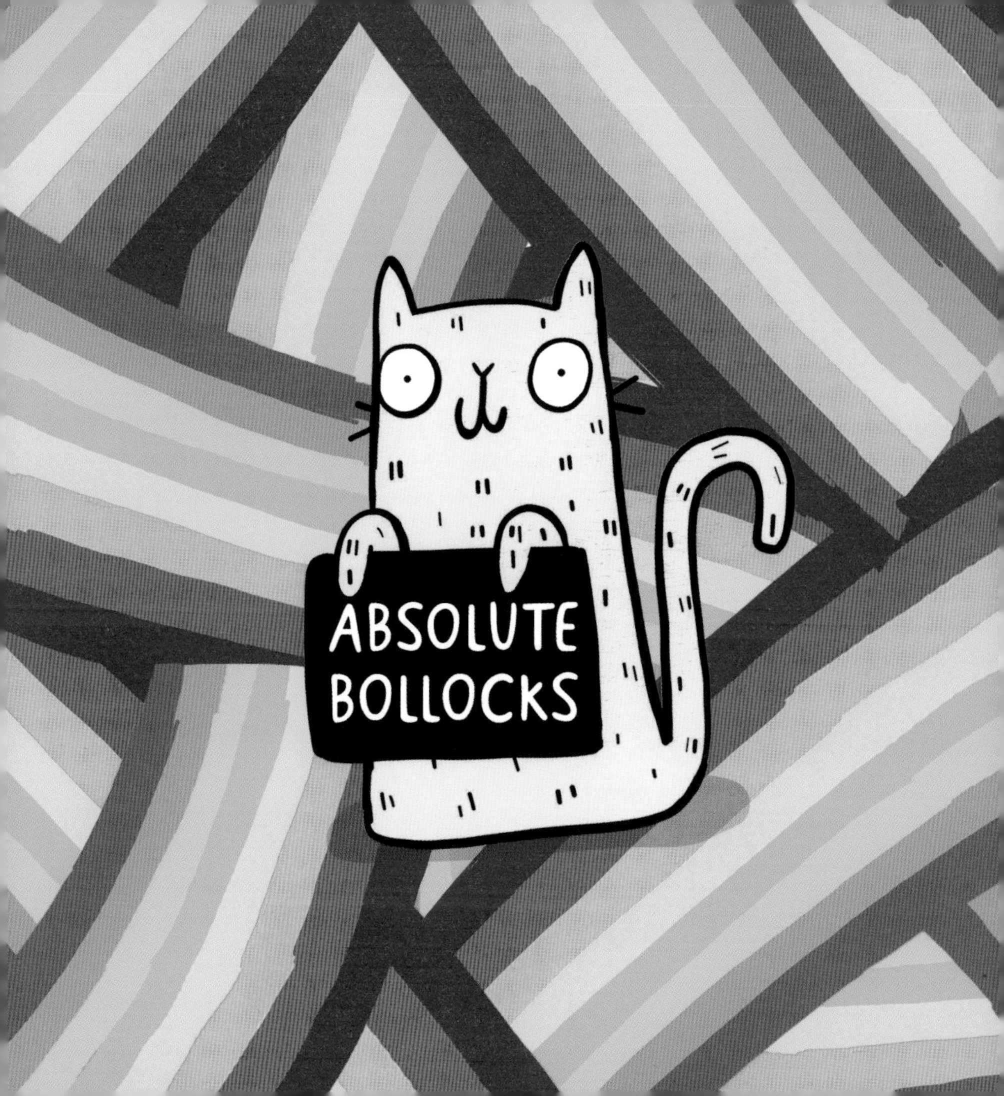
ABSOLUTE BOLLOCKS

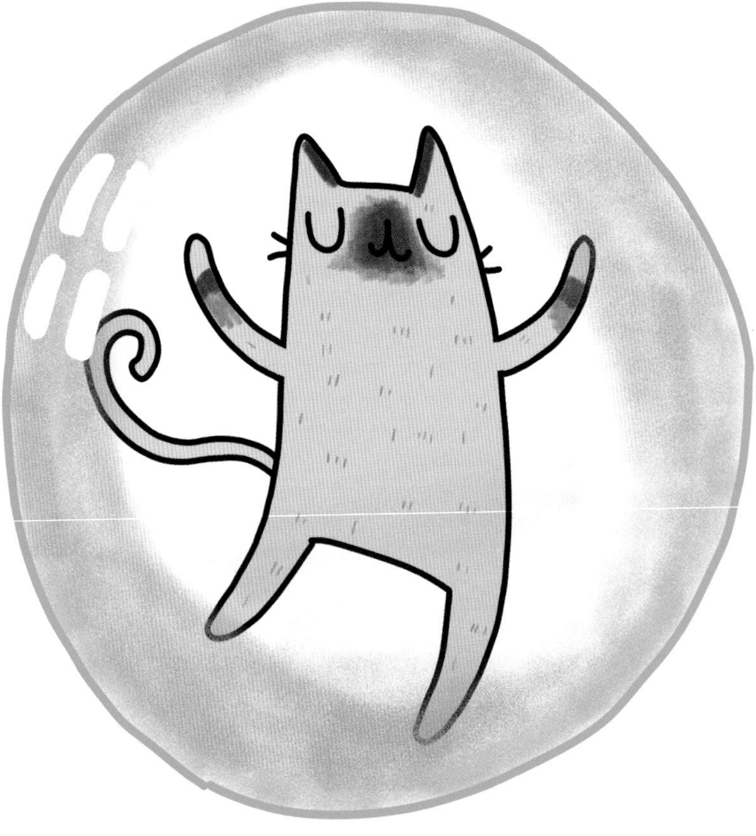

DON'T FUCK WITH MY
FUCKING ENERGY

I'VE GOT BIG PLANS TODAY

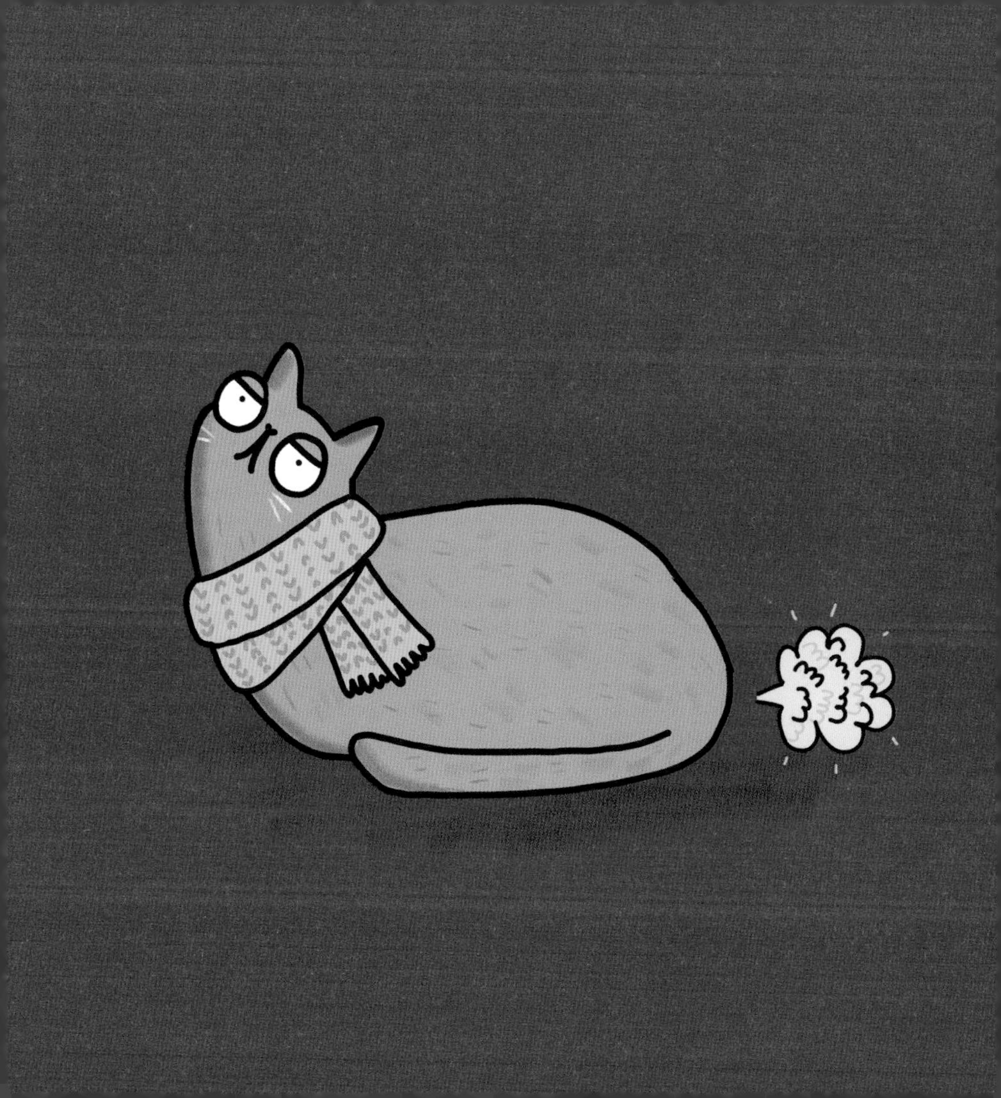

WELL, WOW, I'VE NEVER SEEN
ANYTHING SO FULL OF SHIT

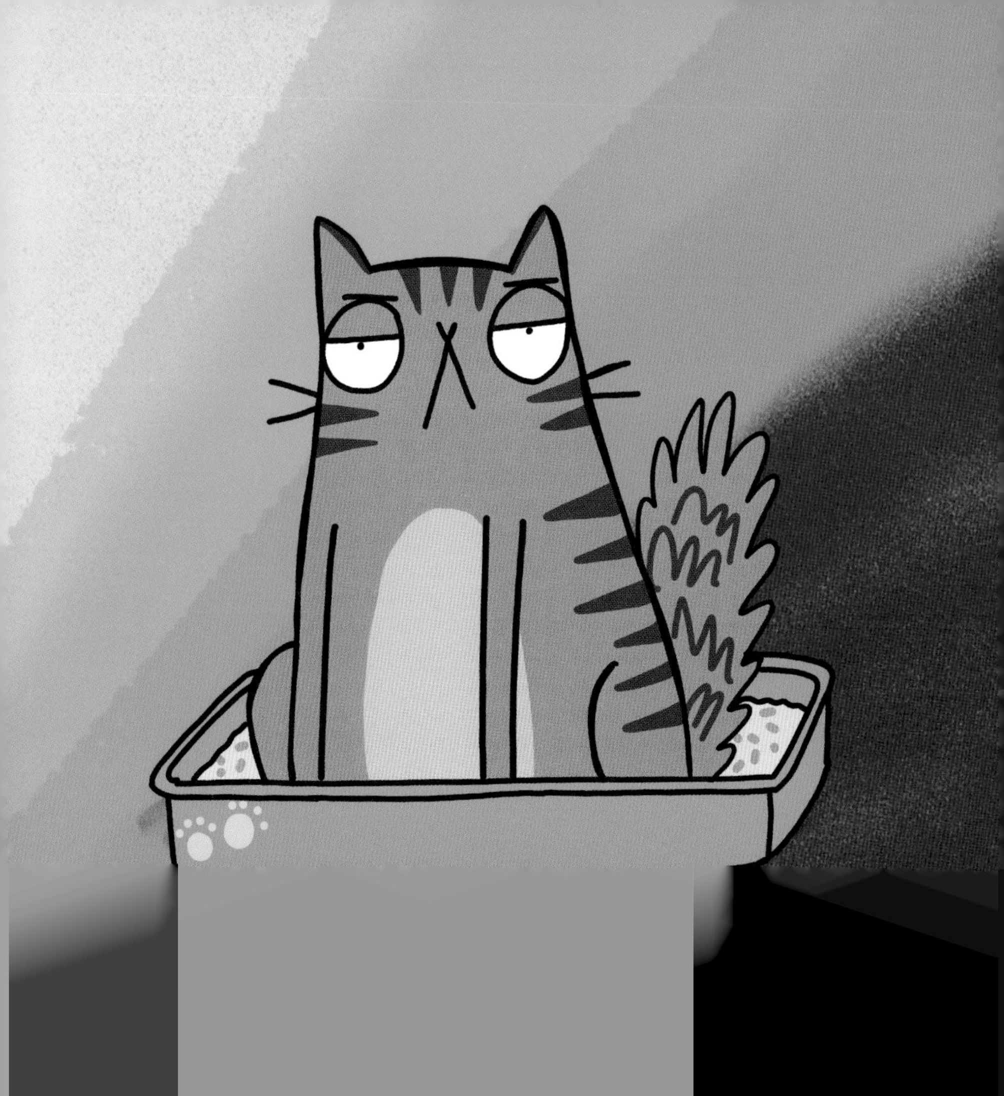

CATS ARE BETTER THAN PEOPLE

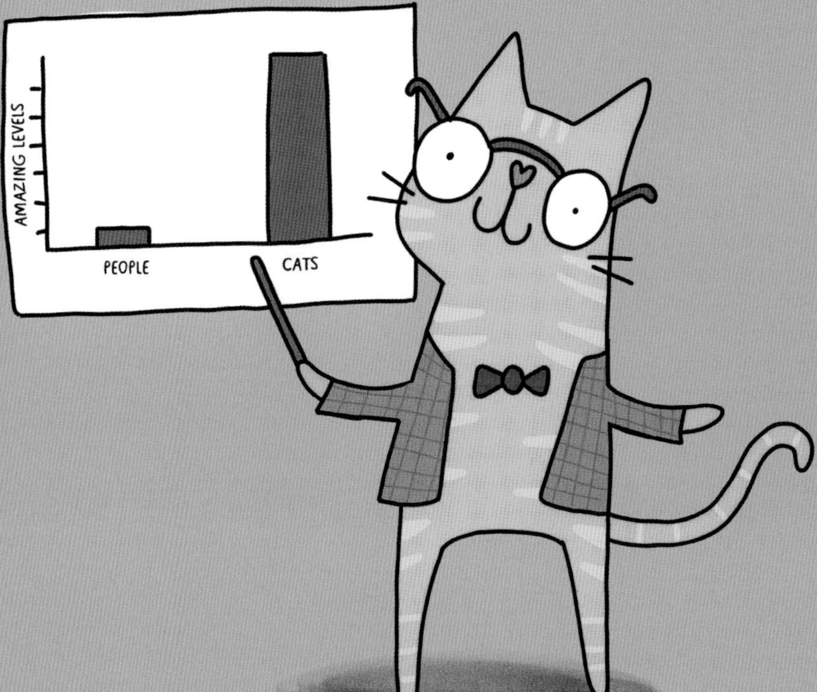
AMAZING LEVELS
PEOPLE
CATS

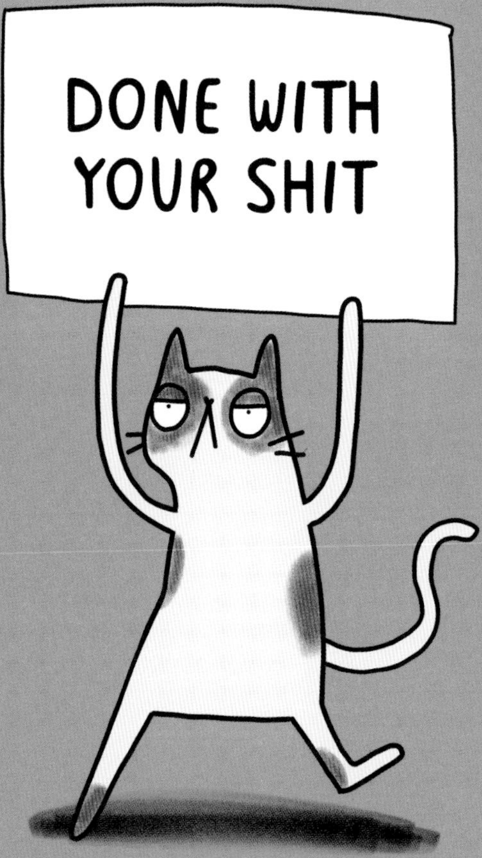
DONE WITH
YOUR SHIT

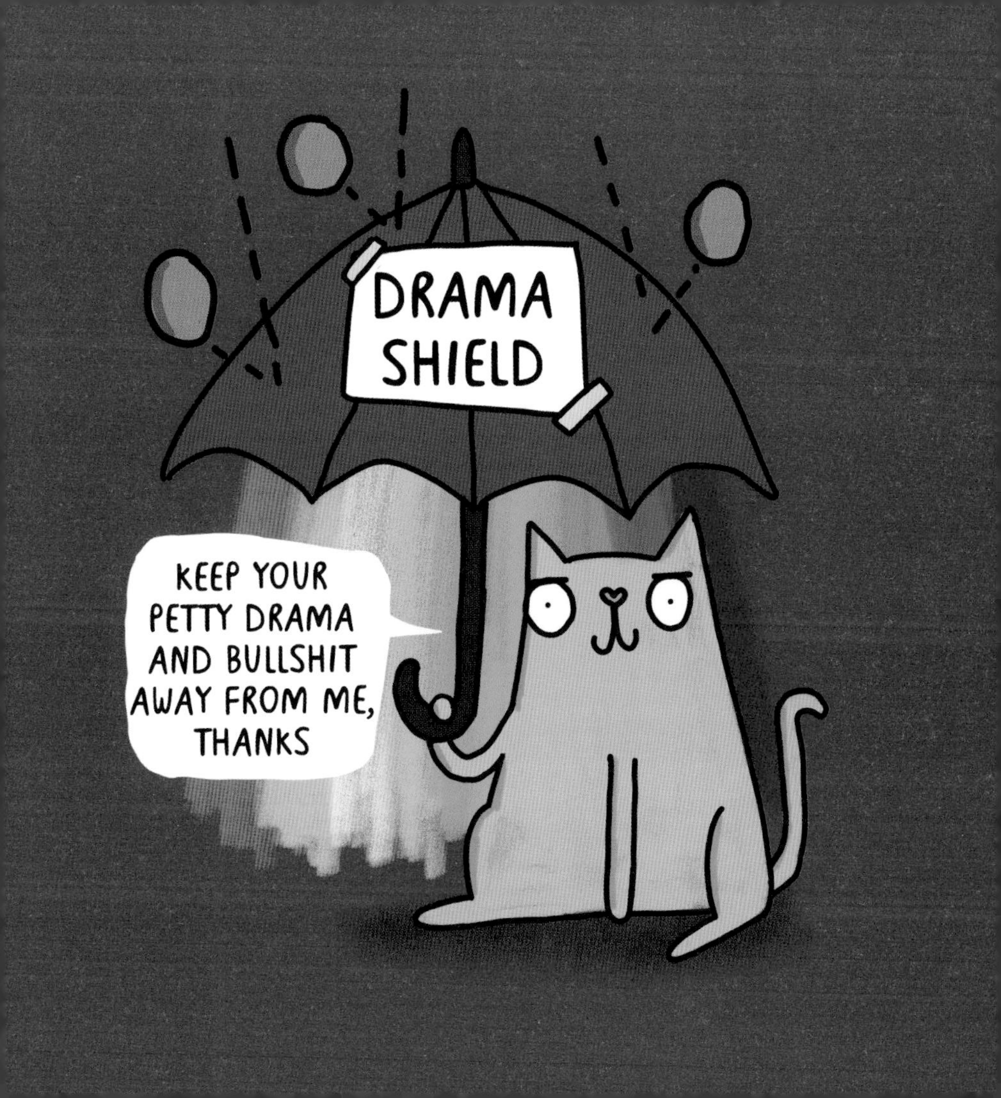
DRAMA SHIELD
KEEP YOUR PETTY DRAMA AND BULLSHIT AWAY FROM ME, THANKS

YOUR NEW CHAPTER
STARTS RIGHT HERE

'NO' IS A FULL SENTENCE

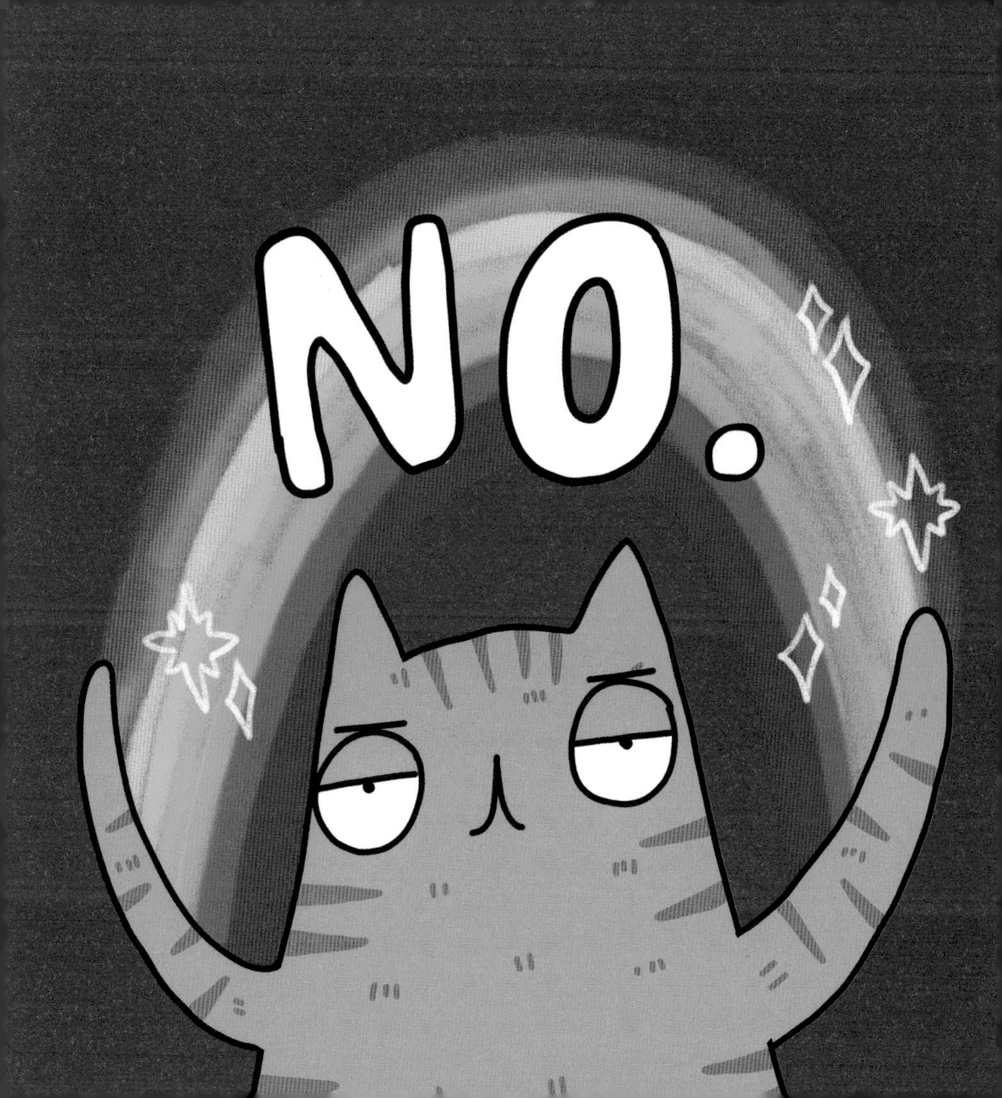
NO.

FLAMIN'GO AWAY

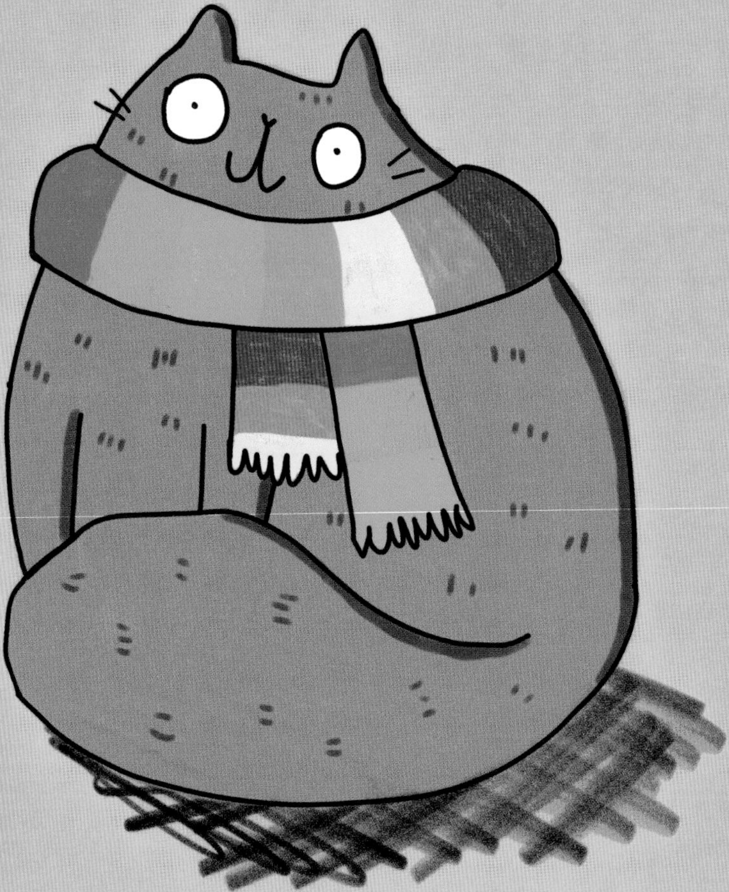

STOP WAITING FOR PURRMISSION TO BE MORE WEIRD. GRANT IT YOURSELF.

DON'T HOLD ONTO THOSE
INTRUSIVE THOUGHTS.
SIEVE THOSE FUCKERS AWAY.
KEEP HOLD OF THE
GOOD SHIT.

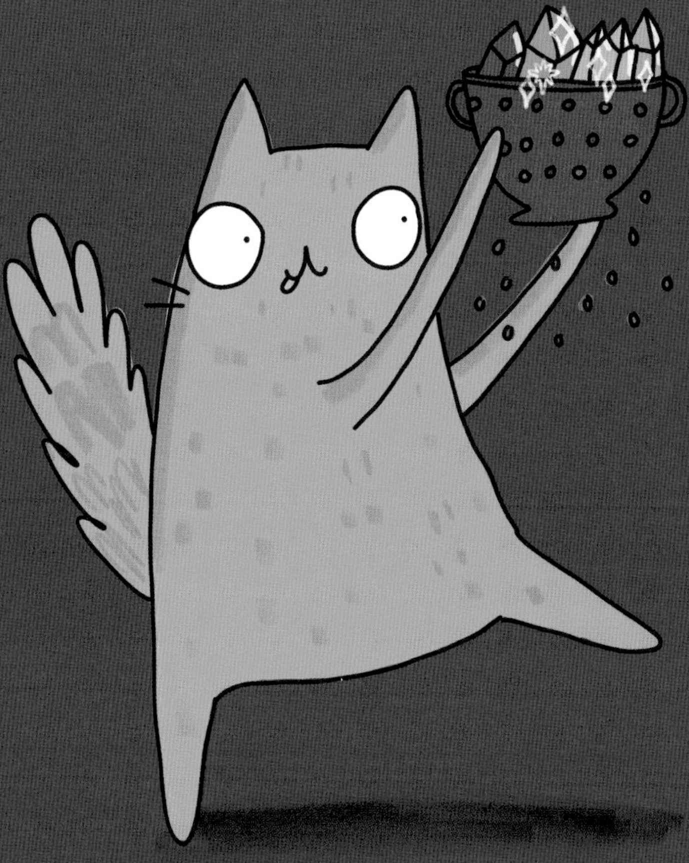

TREAT YO'SELF

SHIT IS GETTING
REAL OUT THERE

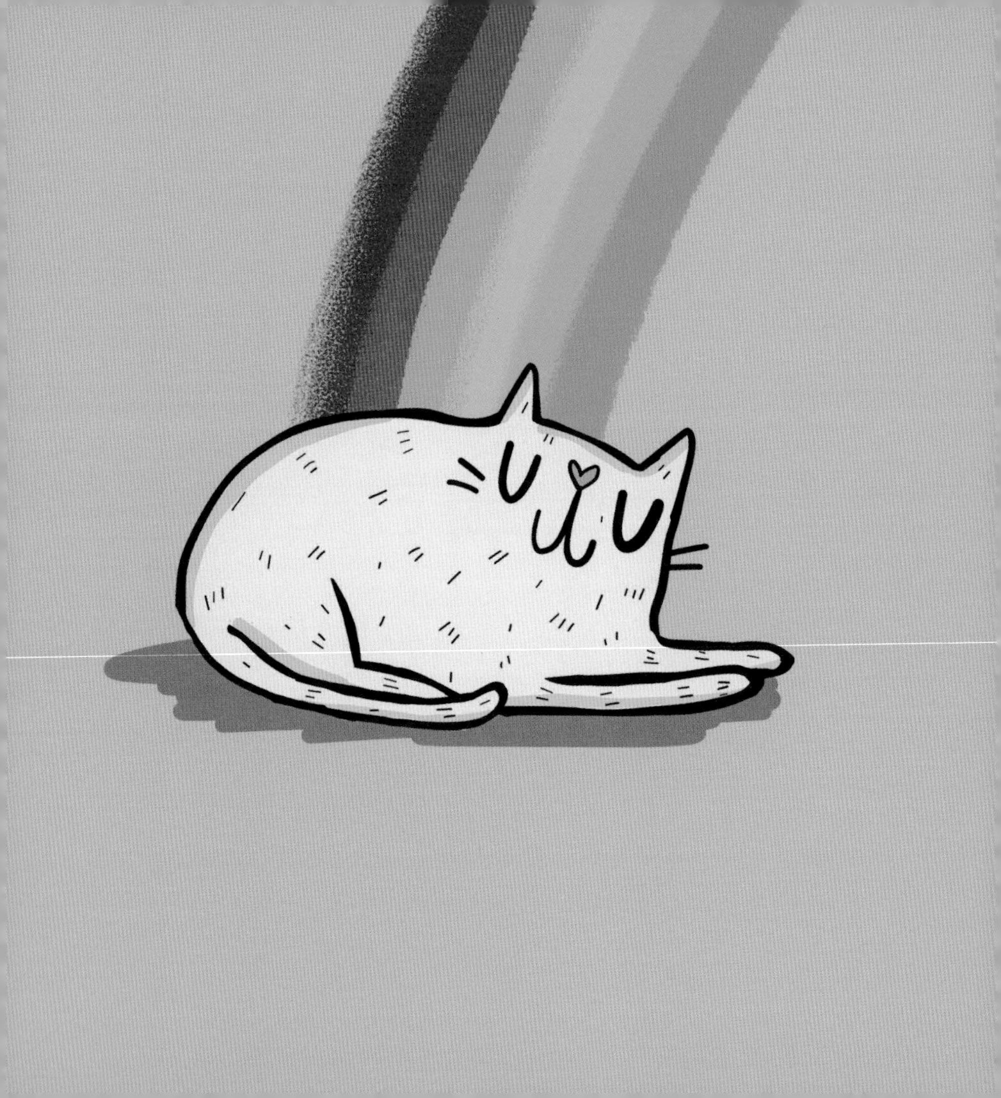

WHEN YOU GET TIRED
LEARN TO REST,
NOT TO QUIT

RECHARGE YOUR BATTERIES,
YOU PIECE OF SHIT

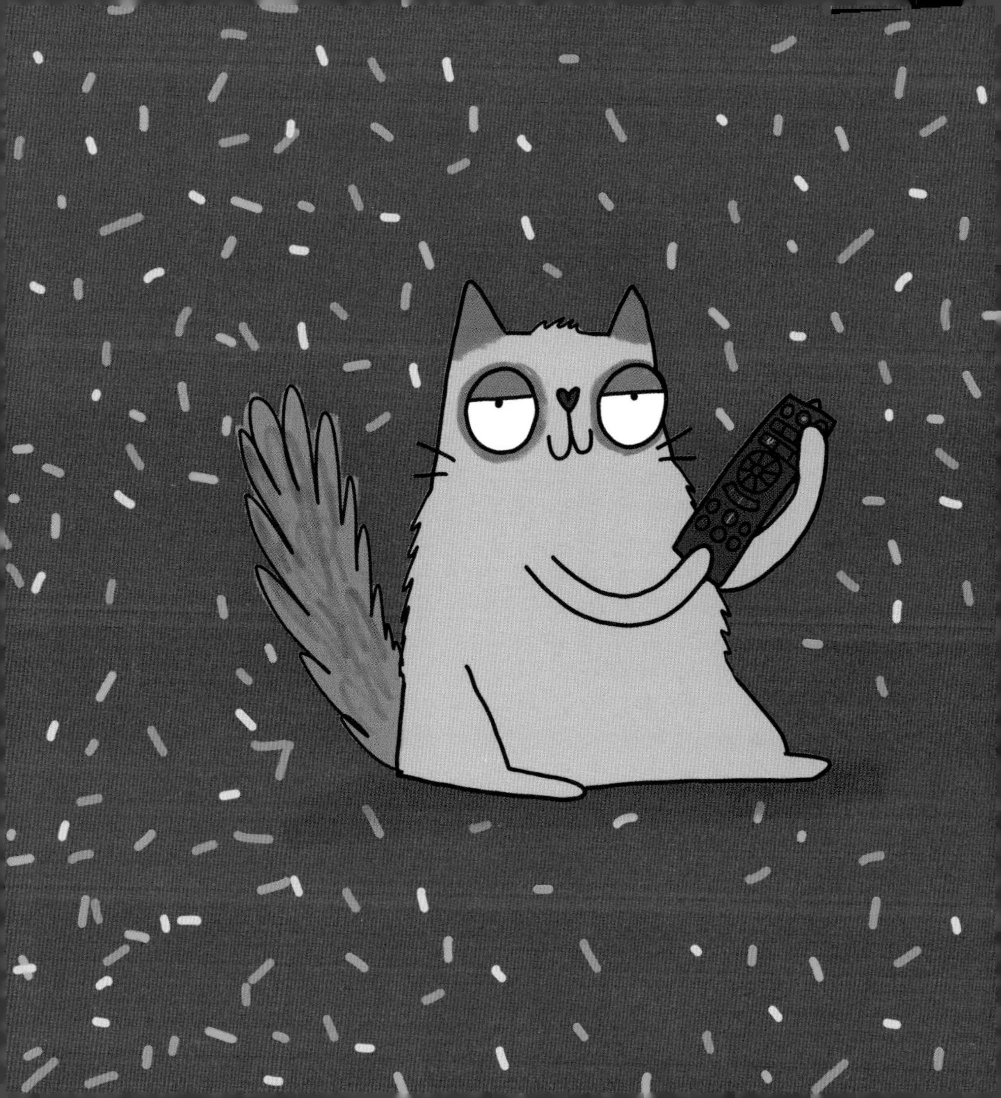

THIS BELL IS FOR
SNACKS, YES?

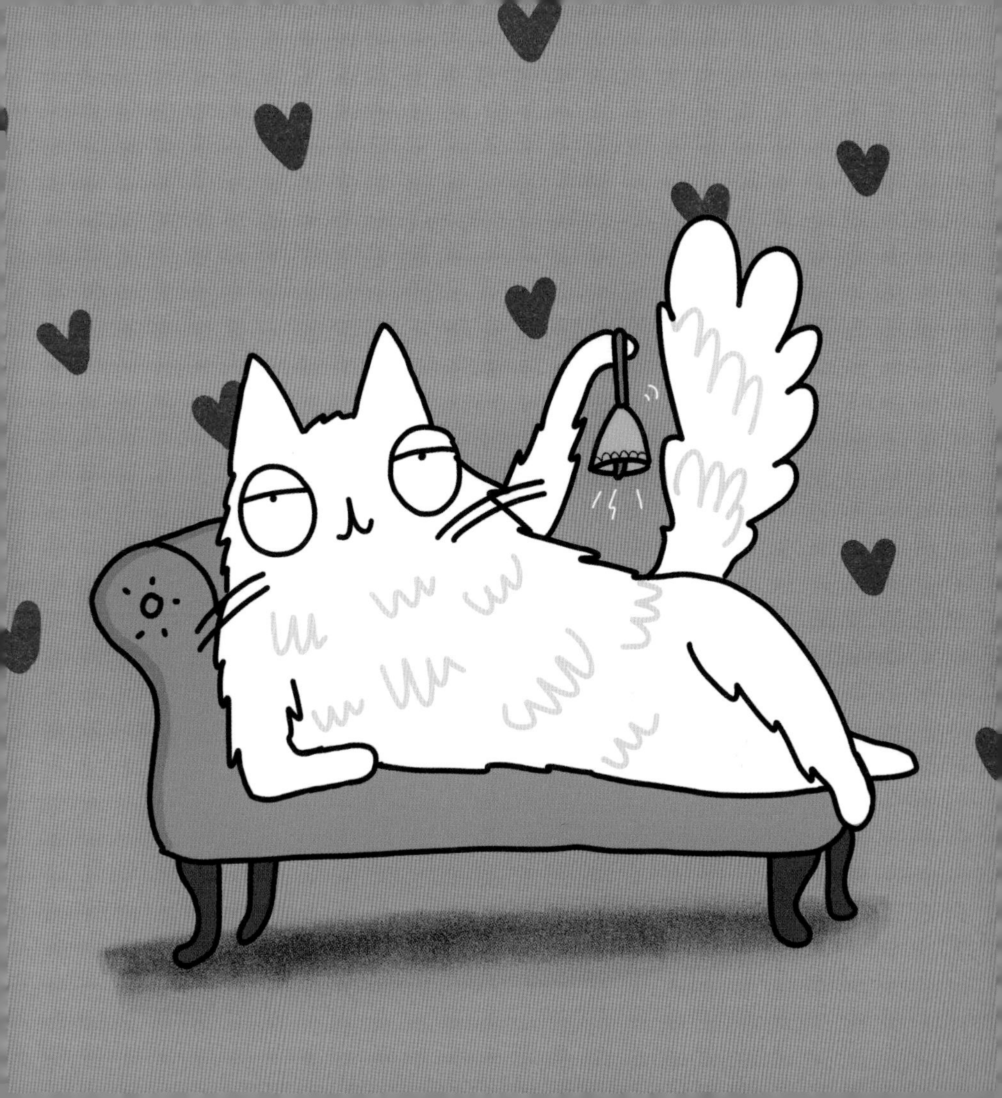

BE PROUD OF YOURSELF FOR
EVERYTHING YOU HAVE
OVERCOME

YOU DON'T HAVE TO PROVE
ANYTHING TO ANYONE

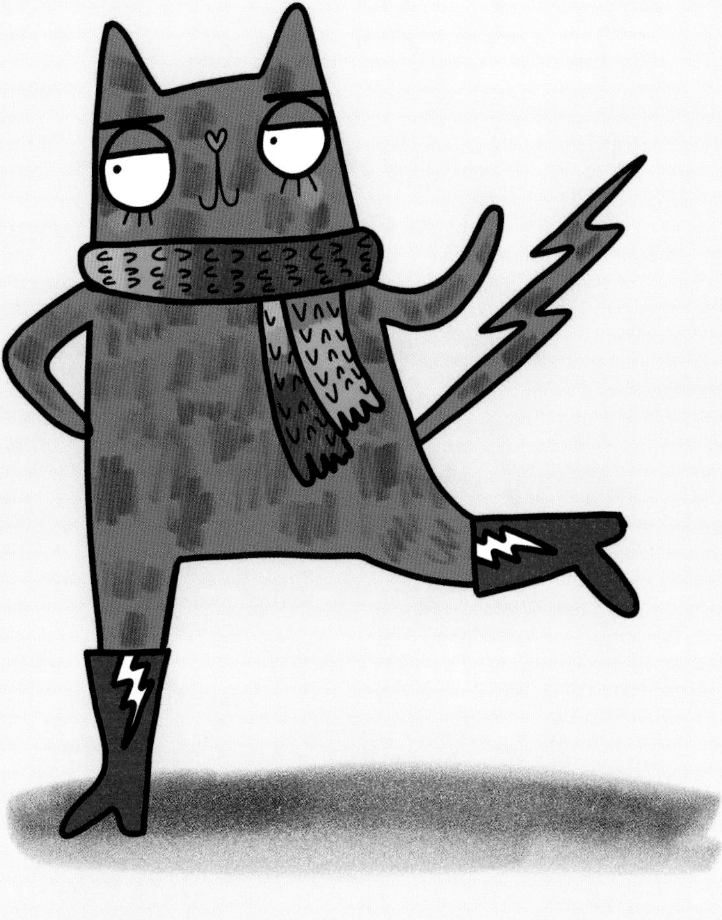

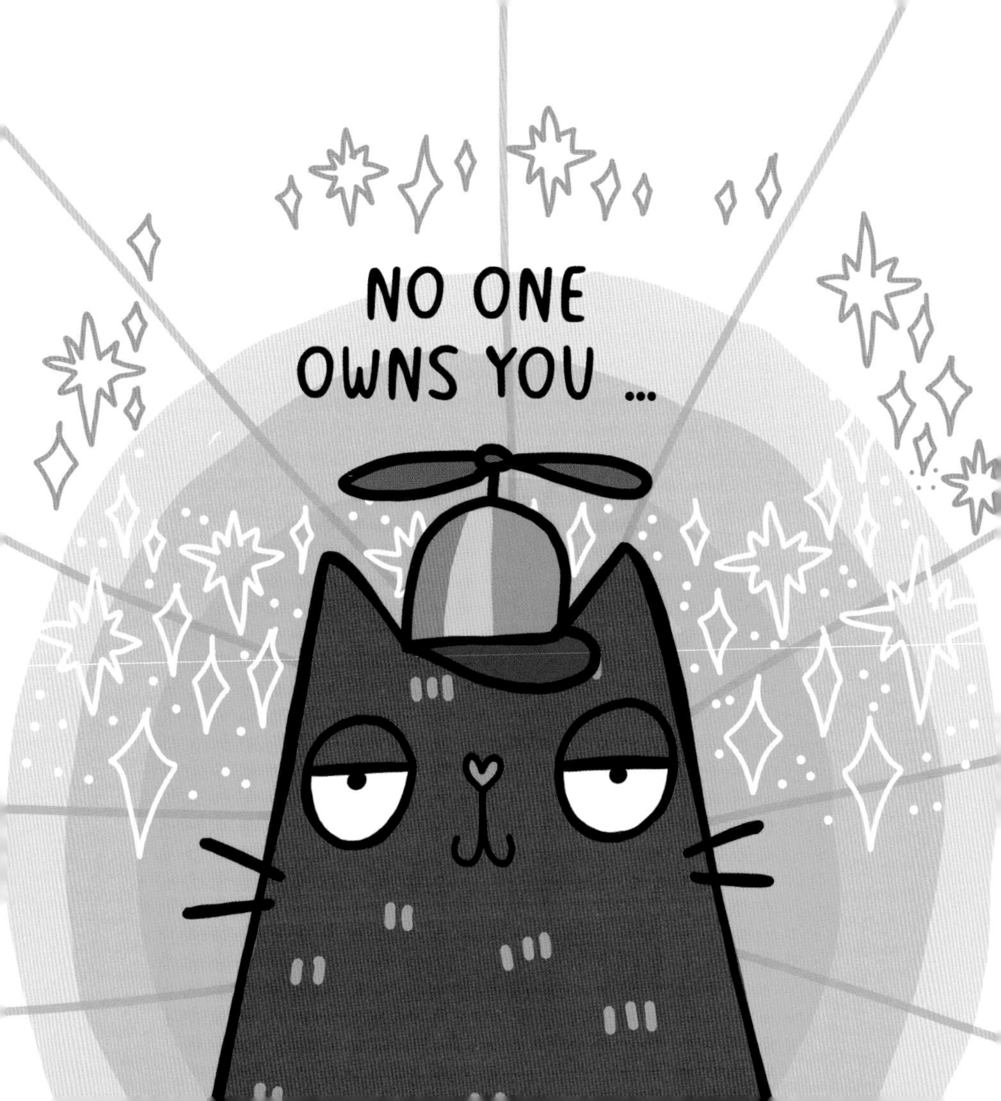
NO ONE
OWNS YOU ...

(APART FROM THOSE LOVELY HUMANS)

THERE IS ONLY SO MUCH
LEMONADE YOU CAN MAKE.
REST.

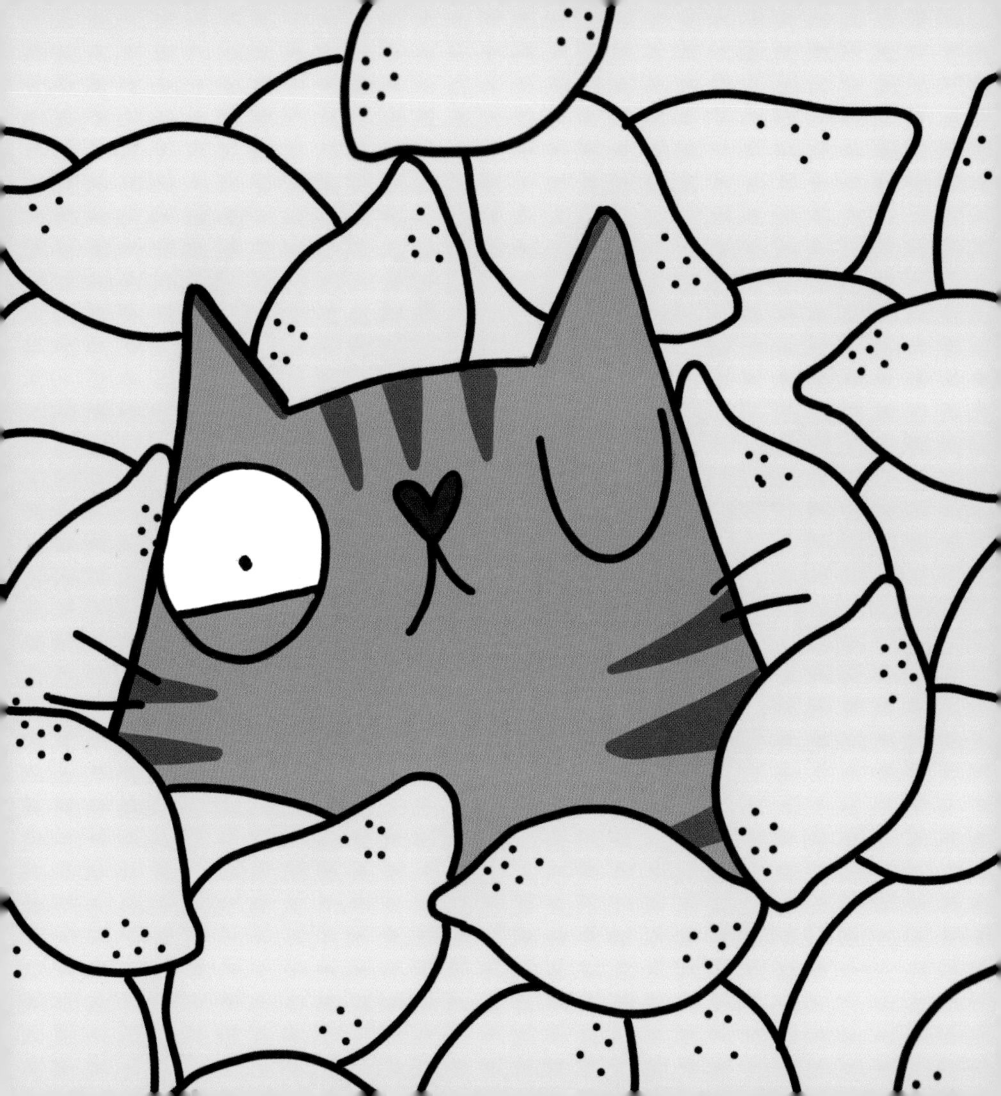

FUCKIN' LOOK
AFTER YOURSELF

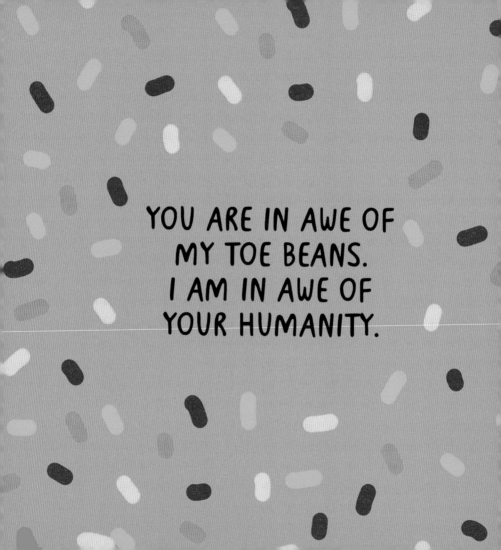

YOU ARE IN AWE OF
MY TOE BEANS.
I AM IN AWE OF
YOUR HUMANITY.

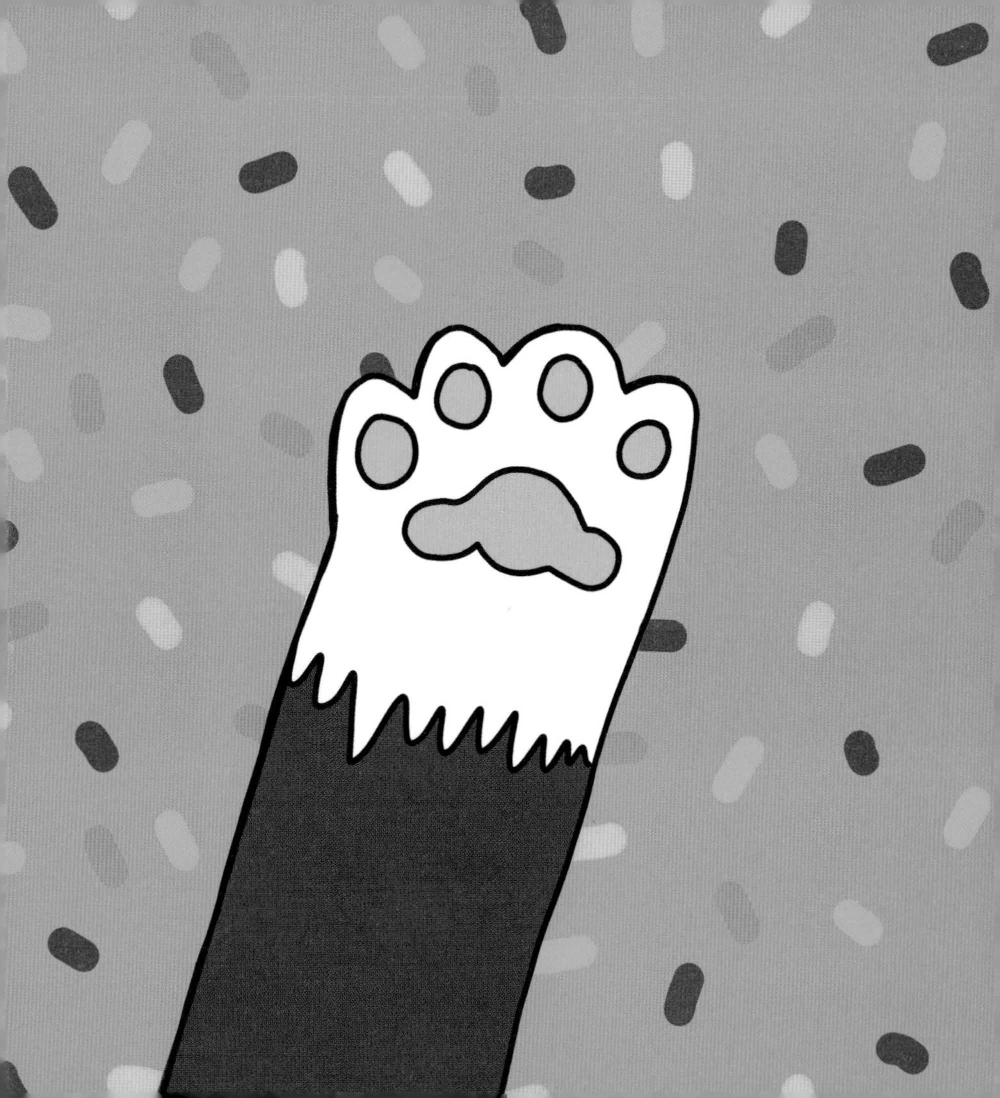

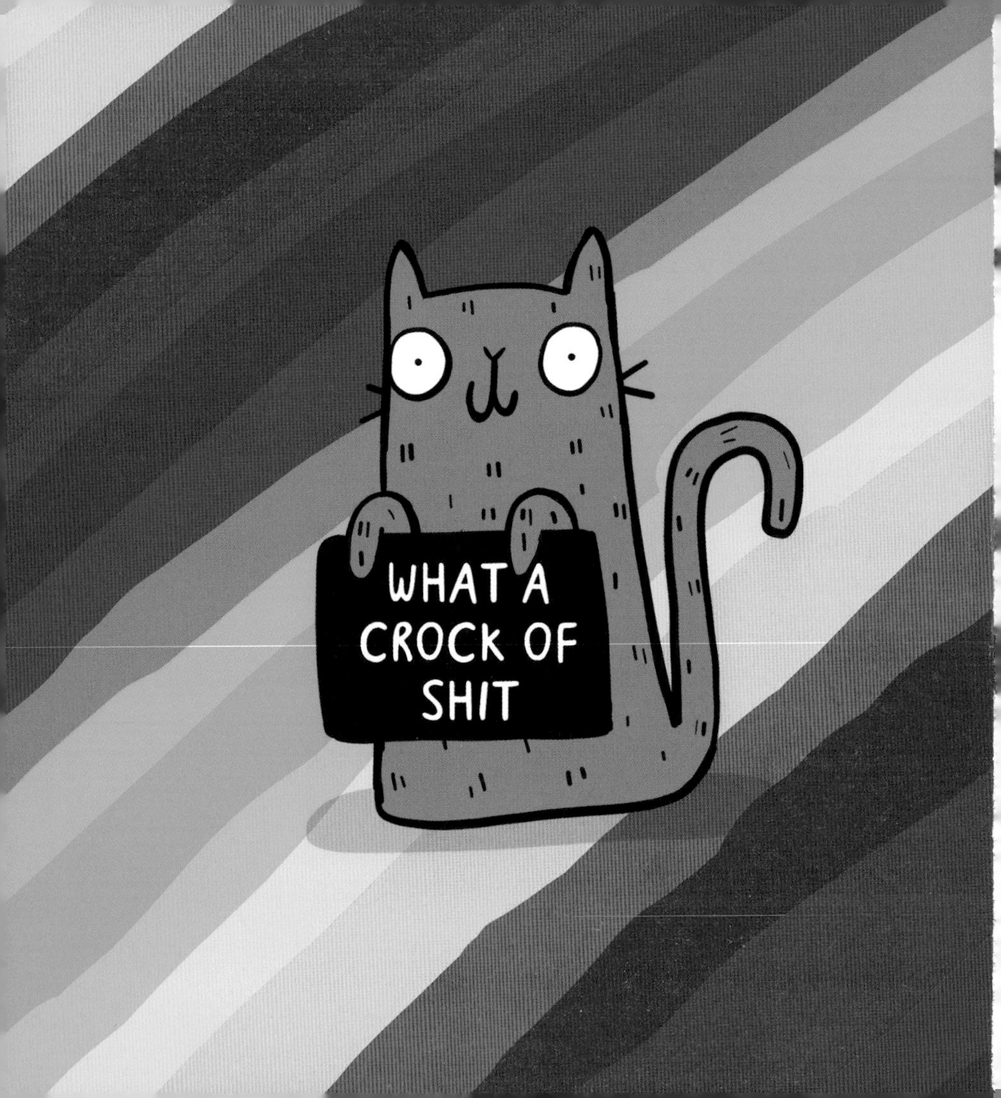
WHAT A
CROCK OF
SHIT